Courage

Under

FIRE

BRANDON JORDAN

COURAGE UNDER FIRE

Copyright © 2021 by Brandon Jordan

ISBN 978-1-952327-36-0

CONTENTS

FOREWORD

I met Brandon Jordan while in prison, at a time when changing my life and becoming someone better than I had been up until that point was of great importance to me. I would later find out in conversation with Brandon, that I was trying to change my life and carry myself a little differently stood out to him. We began to speak to one another, which eventually turned into us having constant conversations about changing our lives and doing better when we got home. Day in and day out, week in and week out, month in and month out, year in and year out this was our topic of conversation.

Courage Under Fire, the first book from Brandon Jordan, chronicles his mindset and journey of prison life from the age of fifteen years old. Taking you from intake as a teenager through the heartache, the laughter, the pain, and the breakthroughs to his release as a man in his mid thirties. Brandon, incarcerated at the tender age of fifteen, showed a level of maturity to what I like to say is "created better where better didn't exist." As you read this book, you'll see the thirst for knowledge that I saw when I met him as a teenager, written with the ability to be raw, soft, passionate, and informative. I'm writing this to you because it is important to me not just because I know Brandon but because the mountains in our lives are to be moved, not solely for our own personal gain, but for others to know that the same is possible in theirs.

—Ed Hennings

PREFACE

The idea for this book came about not only because of my personal life experiences but also due to the principles learned from each of those experiences. I still stand firmly on some of those principles today. Others have been modified and don't hold the same value they once did. Yet they all have played an essential role in shaping who I am not only as a man but as a Black man whose experiences are woven into the fabric of the existence of other Black men and women, courtesy of the environmental conditions that had a hand in creating us all.

The truly interesting thing about life is that there is no manual. I wish I had been equipped for life with instructional paperwork like the kits for the model airplanes I used to build when I was a kid. Honestly, if it had been, it probably wouldn't be as fun: the mess ups, the trial and error, the heartbreaks, and in my case, the laws broken. You see, the paper that came with the model planes says there's only one way to go about building the aircraft for it to look the way it does in the picture on the box. We know there has to be a fuselage, empennage (tail assembly), wings, landing gear, a vertical stabilizer, a spoiler, etc. Without those components, there can be no successful building of the aircraft, model or actual.

But with life there exists no such manual, no "paper." And unlike building an airplane by following instructions, there is no one way to be successful or find happiness. You can literally write your own manual, tailor it to your very own perfect fit, and promulgate it to assist others. So, I named this book *Courage Under Fire* not only because it's the title of one of my favorite songs I've ever written (Check" The Facts of Life" on SoundCloud track 14) but because I know a thing or two about enduring a crucible and remaining steadfast in courage throughout.

Or so it appeared.

I've been to prison four times and in city jails, county jails, detention centers, police districts, boys' homes, group homes, halfway houses—and damn near homeless—all from the ages of fourteen to thirty-four. When I returned home from my last and final prison stint of twelve years, I realized the amount of time I've spent in the system. I went away for the first time at fourteen for a few months, then again at ages fifteen, nineteen, twenty, and twenty-two.

I hate prison, especially the smell of it and how it made me feel. A childlike structure exists there, like the fifteen-to-twenty-minute phone calls that we're allowed and showering with other men. The small cells, the cruel guards (though admittedly not all of them), the senseless rules and racism, the dehumanization, the drab colors of each building. The noises, the warbles of walkie-talkie radios, segregation. The books that you immerse yourself in only to find that the middle pages have been torn out, so you lose interest in finishing. Having to wear other men's underwear! I hate it! I hate it! I hate it! So how the fuck did I end up there four times? That's what I had to figure out: How did I end up back in a place that I hated so much and would tell anyone that with conviction?

I read a book years ago by a holocaust survivor named Victor Frankl that changed the nature and the course of my thinking forever. In *Man's Search for Meaning* Frankl stated, "When we are no longer able to change a situation, we are challenged to change ourselves" (Frankl, 1946). There I sat in 2006, twenty-four years old and eighteen months in on a twenty-year sentence. I knew something had to change. You know why? Because I *hate* prison! I sat for the next decade (I was gone the final time from 2004–2016) looking into myself, trying to get to know myself so well that you'd never be able to tell me something about me that I didn't already know! That was my courage revealing itself under fire of the oppression of the (in)justice system.

I went through every emotion imaginable, including self-hate, resentment, depression, frustration, happiness, and confusion. I had suicidal thoughts. I was just so damn hurt! Sorrowful, angry, anything that else you can think of. Shit, I damn near went crazy from thinking too much. But I figured it's better to think too much than not enough, because after all, not thinking enough about things got me there in the first place. I tried every distraction. Basketball didn't work. Dominoes … nope. Spades … hell no. Horseshoes … never. Talking to people… not at all. Crying… no more tears to give. Exercising… wrong. Jogging… I lost weight too quickly. I'd become ultrathin and sad with no sense of humor.

Nothing worked until I started to look within. I found something in me that I'd never noticed. I was once told by someone that "the greatest beauty lies in uncharted corners of your own existence." That rang true. I began looking deeper and deeper every day. Once I found my courage, the fire I was in didn't seem so hot. So my challenge to you, whoever you are reading this, is to find your courage. It's already there. You must find it, harness, and manifest it. Once you do, only you can stop you. But until you do, you'll continue to allow others to.

As you begin to read this book, know that it only serves as a tool for inspiration. Everything else is up to you! Stay powerful. Stay purposeful. And always stand on principle!

Chapter 1

NO FEAR IS UNCONQUERABLE

I remember when I was a kid, my mom used to always say to me, "It's easy to get in trouble, but ain't no easy out." Truth be told, I didn't know what the hell she was talking about. I was too fixated on doing unnecessary stuff throughout the neighborhood and screaming, "What I do?" whenever I got caught.

I was raised primarily in Milwaukee, Wisconsin, on the 2100 block of North Twenty-Third Street. This neighborhood was dubbed "Little Beirut" in the early 1990s by the Milwaukee Police Department in reference to the siege of Beirut that took place in the summer of 1982 as part of the Lebanon war. I was eight or nine when I used to hear people say, "Lil Beirut." I always thought they were saying "Lil Babe Ruth" after the famed Boston Red Sox player; after all, I was only a grade-schooler.

I was born on an army base in Lawton, Oklahoma. We moved from there to California, where we stayed for a few years. My dad was in the Special Forces, so we went from California to Anchorage, Alaska, and then finally to Milwaukee in 1987 after his discharge.

I admittedly disliked Milwaukee when we first arrived because it was unfamiliar to me. My mom and only brother were born there. My dad is originally from Augusta, Georgia, but had resided in Milwaukee since he was a kid. So in my mind, I was the odd man out. All my cousins on my dad's side and my mom's entire family were born in Milwaukee except for my grandma. Early on, I always felt a little different and out of place. My older brother used to tease and taunt me about not being born there like everyone else. He would tell me that I was adopted and a "country bumpkin" because I was born in Oklahoma. I hated him for that, but in retrospect, he was just being an older sibling, no matter how lousy I thought he was.

Another reason why I disliked our new city was because I started school early in Alaska, in Milwaukee, they put me in my "right" grade. I hated everything about it, so I figured if I *acted out* then my mom would eventually say, "Let's go back to Alaska." Yeah, that shit didn't work. Needless to say, we stayed and I struggled accepting it. I acted out at home, at school, and pretty much everywhere that you could imagine. During my rebellion, my dad wound up with an addiction to crack cocaine. This addiction led my mom to file for divorce in 1991 after a decade of marriage.

We'd just moved from "Little Beirut," although my grandparents and all my cousins were still there, and so was I daily, despite my mother making us leave.

That same year I suffered a near-death experience at home with my brother. At the time, I was deathly afraid of the dark, and my brother knew it. So he would sometimes wrap me in a blanket and drag me around the house as I screamed and struggled unsuccessfully to break loose. This time in particular he wrapped me up and tossed me into my room. I was nine, so he was obviously way stronger than I. Not knowing where I was, all I felt was the blanket loosen. I sprang from it with relief, realized I was in my room, and grabbed the knob on the closed door. It wouldn't twist. Still afraid and in tears, I yelled my brother's name, "Monie!" not knowing it was him holding the knob from the other side. Unaware if he was in the room with me or not, I panicked!

I turned around with my eyes closed, swinging with force! I unfortunately swung too forcefully, knocking myself off balance and into my bedroom window. It broke on impact. In a rage, I hopped up and snatched my arm back to gain my footing. As the jagged glass on the windowsill tore through my flesh down to the bone, my arm went numb immediately. The glass was so sharp I didn't feel myself get cut.

I looked down as the flesh on my arm opened in a bloom-like state, similar to a time-lapse video of the maturation of a flower. I saw my bone, and I screamed, *"MONIE!"* My brother must have detected the desperation in my tone because without hesitation he came rushing in. He looked shocked when he caught sight of my arm still pumping blood with every vein, artery, and tendon cut, spewing blood profusely with a limp arm that was only attached by bone. He wrapped my arm with a towel; the towel was soaked with blood immediately like one square of one-ply toilet paper in a torrential downpour. He went to get another one . . . same result. By that time, I was losing consciousness from so much blood lost. He got another towel, and it seemed as if they were beginning to work, but we were wrong.

Monie held onto my arm and led me outside where a police car happened to be stuck in rush hour traffic directly in front of our house. He flagged the officers down after sitting me on the curb. It was August 1991, and the sun was draining whatever life I had left out of me. The police came over to me as they dispatched an ambulance. I remember repeatedly saying, "I gotta get out the sun." My brother helped carry me from the curb to our sunporch, where I fainted once he placed me on the ground. He slapped me to keep me alert. I told him, 'I'm sleepy, Monie," not knowing that the feeling of sleepiness was imminent death.

He never let me go to sleep, thankfully. The ambulance finally came, and the EMT placed a tourniquet on my arm to suppress the bleeding. It worked well enough to get me to the hospital, courtesy of her holding my arm the entire ride. My mom ran from her job at the courthouse two to three blocks up to the hospital I was initially taken to. I'd lost over half the blood in my body by the time she'd got to me at Mt. Sinai Hospital. My dad was there, as well as my brother. The doctors wouldn't let me look at my arm as I lie on the gurney, watching them carry in bins of blood packs to replenish my body. My parents and brother stood in a corner in the distance, staring helplessly. I looked over to put my thumb up as I said, "I'll be okay, Ma," something my dad used to always do and say when he wanted me to worry less. Unbeknownst to me, my life hung in the balance. I just didn't want her to worry.

The physician asked me, "Are you ready to go to sleep?" Before I could answer, he said, "1 . . . 2 . . . 3 . . . goodnight," and I was out.

I awoke eleven and a half hours later with 330 stitches; 230 were internal and one hundred external. The doctors told my mom I'd never be able to use my right arm again. Fortunately, I write this with the same arm and hand that were severely damaged. My brother was ecstatic that I'd survive. To prevent him from getting into any trouble, we made up a story instead of telling my parents what really happened.

For the next few years, I endured physical therapy and learned to do everything with my left hand. Then I had to relearn to do things with my right hand. I'd become circumstantially ambidextrous. I learned to like it. The ironic thing about me surviving such a traumatizing and near-tragic occurrence is that my paralyzing fear of the dark seemed to have diminished. As a matter of fact, from that point forward, I seemed to have lost the basic human mechanism, the need for fear.

The thing about fear is that at the basic level, it guides our fight or flight responses and pretty much helps us with preparation in many cases. After my accident, I seemed to have developed the urge to welcome danger and all things potentially harmful. I was no longer afraid of the dark. I would sit still alone in my room with no lights or TV. I began hanging out in the basement, a place I had vowed never to go without light.

It was uncanny. The word *fearless* had taken on new meaning. Typically, I understood the notion of being fear less to mean experiencing fear yet being compelled to move beyond it via courage; hence, the idiom, If you fake your fear, your fear will disappear. I no longer experienced any fear to face. I became extremely daring, reckless, even borderline suicidal. I can remember hearing someone say about God, "If you ask, you shall receive." Me being an antagonistic asshole, I decided to test that theory via prayer. Yes, I literally prayed to die at fourteen years old. Simply to see if it would happen. As foolish as it sounds, I really wanted to know if what I was told was true. Not dying after the accident was my earliest recollection of questioning what was deemed important—God. It was the beginning of an uncanny self-belief that over time became difficult for me to explain.

Never Stop Moving

When I was eleven years old, my stepdad, who spent some time in the navy, would take my brother and me over to his mother's apartment complex to swim, hang in the Jacuzzi, and have fun overall. I didn't know how to swim. I was so inexperienced with swimming that I wouldn't even take my shoes off. Poolside one day, my stepdad, Carl, convinced me to take my shoes off, put on my swim trunks, and as he said, "Come hang out by the pool." I figured, *Okay, why not?*

As soon as I relaxed mentally and felt safe enough to walk around with the least bit of confidence, I felt a forceful shove on my back. As I went flying into the water in a split second, I held my breath and closed my eyes before I became submerged in what I thought was the deep end. I could hear muffled laughter from everyone who'd seen what happened. As I waited to resurface, for some reason, I never panicked. In that moment, I'd again experienced a sense of calm as I conquered another fear of mine. I heard my stepdad yell, "Bran, don't stop moving!"

I thought about all the movies I'd seen when people swam underwater so gracefully that they seemed to be one with the ocean (or in my case, pool) eyes open, body undulating in a mermaid-like fashion. I tried it to no avail as my knee hit the bottom of the pool. The water I was in was four feet deep, and I was taller than that. The chlorine burned my eyes as they opened, and I eventually stood up.

I did listen to Carl, though. I did not stop moving. I eventually learned how to swim, not that day exactly, but I got there. What I did realize that day was that I often overthought things that were simple and made them much more complicated than they had to be. My stepdad taught me to never stop moving in that water and in life. I can't tell you how many things I've faced in life that I would've bet my life on that I wasn't ready for, but somehow I rose to the occasion and weathered every storm.

The thing, or predicament, that I don't believe anyone can ever truly prepare for is prison. There is no surefire way to prepare to have all your rights stripped away from you. I was just fifteen years old when I experienced it.

It was February 2, 1997, roughly 11:30 p.m., when my cousin and I were in Lil Beirut, renamed "the ghetto" by my generation. I had been robbed at gunpoint earlier in the winter while out with my girlfriend and her niece. They took my money and left the guy next to us at the bus stop standing in a puddle of melted snow after taking his shoes! I was vengeful and angry after that.

From that point on, my cousin and I went on a robbing spree that led to February 2nd. The foolish thing about this spree is that it was totally random. If we thought you had it, we wanted it, and we were taking it. We were young, brash, and arrogant, armed, and equipped with an utter disregard for human life that meant we would take yours and put ours on the line without hesitation. The funny thing about that night is, we were only walking to the gas station until we spotted a potential victim. The danger of committing random actions is that they are met with deliberate reactions and consequences. What my cousin didn't know was that I'd planned on shooting whoever I pulled the gun on that night. He was along for that life-changing ride.

We saw someone walking. I pulled the gun out immediately; it was already cocked and ready. We used to wear ski masks in the winter rolled up like skull caps in case anything went down. After I pulled the gun, I rolled my mask down. We pushed him into a nearby alley, and I ordered him to get to his knees after facing him away from me. I took his coat off him and threw it aside. I told him, "If you move, I'm poppin' you." (*Pop* is a street term for shoot or being shot.)

My cousin went through the guy's pockets and came up with absolutely nothing! I was pissed. In my mind, he moved. I shot. Reality set in immediately after I had pulled the trigger. My cousin said, "B.J., let's go!" He grabbed his coat, and we ran off in a panic, adrenaline pumping in a state of shock, so much so that I had not even put the gun away as we ran.

I just shot somebody . . . I just shot somebody! That statement echoed loud in my head like a baritone voice in an empty hallway as we walked into my aunt's house trying to act as normal as possible. We sat in the living room as we heard sirens in the distance, more than likely rushing to the crime scene. I was nervous. Uncertain as to what would happen. Intrigued.

Uneasy, but not as afraid as I probably should have been.

It was a Sunday when this happened. We were taken into custody four days later on February 6. My dad was the one who brought the police to my location, because according to them I was "armed and dangerous," so they may approach with caution and aggression. In other words, they were more than willing to shoot once they caught me, fifteen years old or not.

I was upstairs with my older cousins in a known drug house, watching *The Nutty Professor*, when my dad walked in and said, "Bran, the police are outside. They wanna talk to you."

I looked at him surprised. "The police?" I questioned inquisitively.

My cousins questioned in unison, "Why you bringing them here?"

To prevent the police from coming in to get me, I walked out with my dad, because nobody else needed to go to jail on account of my defiance. I walked outside cautiously because the police had (have) a reputation of shooting without warning. They had killed my cousin's father two years prior, so that was in my young mind as I took what wound up being life-changing steps.

I made it outside, looked around, and saw nobody. I turned to my dad, curiosity commandeering my face and said, "Where they at?"

He didn't verbally respond, but I did notice him glance across the street to an empty parking lot that was partially illuminated by a streetlight. It belonged to what used to be a local restaurant that then stood dilapidated and alone. I noticed multiple figures slowly emerge from behind the building (it was like I was in a movie). My cousins and uncle stood watching from the porch and doorway with bated breath to see what was about to happen.

I could tell by their gait as the police came toward me that they didn't want to simply talk, as my dad had initially said. My first inclination was to run, so I did. My dad grabbed me, holding on to me firmly between his arms as he gripped the chain link fence behind me that surrounded my cousin's grandma's house. Before I knew it, I was surrounded by plainclothes officers with badges dangling from their necks.

My dad stepped away as they put their hands on me. I looked at him with an expression that screamed, *Help me*. I'd become a child again in that moment. One officer said to me, "We just wanna talk to you downtown for a little while." As he guided me into the back seat of a detective car without cuffs. He turned to my dad and said, "You can come with him, Mr. Jordan, because he is a minor."

I was looking out of the window from the backseat, and pretty much waiting for my dad to say okay and get in with me. He never did. I heard him reply, "I have something to take care of."

I was devastated. My heart sank as he walked away from the squad car, waving goodbye but saying, "See you later. Daddy loves you." His words and actions did not coincide. I stared out of the window for as long as I could see him as they drove me away from freedom. I changed windows as the car turned the corner. I was on my knees looking out the back window as my dad wound up farther and farther in the distance.

I heard the officer say, "Sit down, Brandon," in a surprisingly soft and almost empathetically parental tone. After a brief hesitation, I turned and sat, heartbroken as I stared down at the Carolina blue Dickies I was wearing. I didn't know what was to come. I'd never known fear and loneliness on such a profound level until that moment. Unbeknownst to me, it would get deeper.

We pulled up to the city jail downtown, a place I'd only heard stories about, also a place I never thought that I would see in real life. Damn, was I wrong. The officers escorted me from the squad car to an obscure elevator in a poorly lit, morgue-ish parking garage that reeked of a combination of cheap cologne, faux leather, metal, and cold stone. I was numb. I walked with my head down the entire time. It did not feel real. I was in a state of shock. I kept thinking, *I got school tomorrow.*

They took my picture, well, mug shot, made me face left, then right, then forward. They fingerprinted me and handcuffed me to a cold hardwood bench. I was not there long before they uncuffed me and escorted me to a small windowless room with a table and two chairs, one on each side. I sat alone momentarily before two detectives walked in, one with a semisolemn look, the other one not so much. *Good cop, bad cop,* I was guessing.

The solemn cop asked, "What happened on the night of February second?"

I lied. "I don't know."

"Come on now," he retorted as the other cop rifled through my coat pockets from across the room. He found an unspent bullet I'd put there and forgot about. They continued to question me. I continued to lie, not necessarily out of principle but some weird combination of fear and logic. My thoughts were, *If they know what they claim, then they probably wouldn't be asking me questions.* But on the flipside, if I said something, they would definitely know.

They offered me cigarettes, sodas, something from McDonalds, and more cigarettes. I accepted it all and still would not talk to them. They never Mirandized me. Although I had no knowledge of Ernesto Miranda's 1966 case and eventual Supreme Court decision that said criminal suspects must be informed of their right against self-incrimination and their right to consult an attorney before being questioned by police, I did know from watching TV shows that they typically say something along the lines of "You have the right to remain silent . . . and anything you say can and will be held against you, etc." Plus, I was fifteen years old, a minor, and not one officer contacted my parents, partially because my dad walked away from me while I was in that squad car and partially because they wanted to keep the suspect that they had in custody, in custody.

Eventually they left the room for a few minutes before returning with a yellow stationery pad. One of them sat (the "good cop") while the other one stood with his back up against the far wall and his arms crossed. The good cop looked at the yellow pad intently and asked, "Do you know ___?" (He said my cousin's name.) I tried as hard as I could to keep a straight face as I mustered the word, no. It was filled with deceit and lacked conviction. He stared at me blankly in disbelief and asked me again, more deliberately this time with a slightly elevated tone, "*Do you know ___?*"

I nervously replied, "I don't know who you talkin' 'bout," as I slightly fidgeted in my seat because I knew exactly who they were referring to. I just didn't know how *they* knew.

The good cop said, "Okay," then looked at the pad and commenced to read off a detailed account of the events of that night. I was shocked. *How did they know? Where is my cousin?* It all hit me at once. That is when the real fear set in. I had come to realize later that my cousin had been taken into custody hours before me, they knew all along what had happened, and that I was lying about everything they had asked. They knew we were cousins; they knew I had pulled the trigger! And they knew that they didn't just "wanna talk" as they had initially claimed.

After hours of being interrogated, I was transferred to the juvenile detention facility, where I was finally allowed to call my mom and stepdad. They were in a state of shock and disbelief when I told them why I was in custody. The first thing my mom said was, "They have the wrong person!"

I peeped over my shoulder at the staff member sitting behind me to see how much attention he was paying me, not much it appeared. Then I solemnly whispered into the receiver, "No, they don't, Ma."

"*What!* Where you at?"

I told her. I could hear her waking my stepdad to tell him what was taking place. I just held the phone as tears rolled down my cheeks. I was in a daze for a minute until the staff member's voice jarred me from my reverie. "Jordan, your time is up." I told my mom I had to go.

She said, "Wait, wait! When can I come see you?!"

"I don't know." I replied.

She said, "Okay, find out, and I'll be there as soon as I can."

"Okay," I responded.

I heard her say in a deliberate and heartfelt tone, "I love you, Bran."

Through tears I said, "I love you too, Ma."

That was the beginning of the longest walk that I would ever have to total freedom, a journey that would be filled with so many lessons that no curriculum in school could ever compare.

While I languished in a concrete and metal-filled room in detention, lonely and heartbroken, I was unaware of the political climate in the country at the time. It was February 1997, three months after reelection of the "tough on crime" president William Jefferson Clinton, and I was swept into the current of what they referred to as SJO (serious juvenile offender), a pretty large group of youths, mainly black and brown, whom they chose to use as examples through long prison sentences in a failed attempt to deter other youths from committing crimes.

The SJO approach was part of the Violent Crime Control and Law Enforcement Act of 1994, dubbed "the Clinton crime bill," which was signed into law by Bill Clinton on September 13, 1994, and coauthored by then senator and now 2020 presidential candidate Joe Biden. This bill helped create what we now know as mass incarceration (For an in-depth treatment of the effect of this act, see the *The New Jim Crow* by Michelle Alexander).

There were definitely pros and cons to the bill as with anything. For instance, the bill provided huge amounts of funding for police, who were not all depraved, although it may seem that way at times. One hundred thousand police officers were funded, and about fourteen million dollars at that time for community policing, which can never completely be a bad thing. If and when the relations of the Black community and law enforcement are peaceful and harmonious, if and when. The bill also enacted the Violence Against Women Act, which provided funding to protect women against domestic violence and other crimes. Those are just to name a few of the pros. The most detrimental and pernicious provision of that bill was its twelve million dollars allocated to states around the country to enact what they called "truth in sentencing laws." That piece of funding allowed each state to increase the number of prison beds for individuals convicted of violent crimes who were to serve 85 percent of whatever sentence was given. That provision disproportionately affected black and brown people across the board. Part of the reason it is still discussed today is because the federal government subsidized states across the country to build more prisons. Some were even built but never actually occupied.

So I sat in that room, reading an article in *The Source* magazine about the death of the Notorious B.I.G., six months after Tupac's. The article talked about how the state of hip-hop needed to change because it was becoming too dangerous, too serious, too this or too that, how it was destroying the minds of our youth with all the misogyny, misandry, materialism, glorification of violence, etc. What really needed to change because it was the same that they described hip-hop as, was the judicial system that we all lived under.

They waived me into adult court the following month. At court the judge said to me, "Brandon, you are very intelligent, you're articulate, and you speak very well. Do you understand?"

"Yes."

"So, I believe that you knew what you were doing." Then he spoke at me somewhat by saying, "I'm going to waive this case into the adult system, so he is going to be transferred to the county facilities once a bed is available." The judge banged his gavel onto the sounding block and stated sternly, "Detained!"

Court was how I found out what the hell detained meant, not even realizing that detention, where I resided, was the act of being detained. Ironic, right?

At fifteen years old on April 22,1997, I was transferred from the juvenile detention facility to the Milwaukee County Jail to be tried as an adult in court. My official charge was attempted homicide and armed robbery with an enhancer because I was wearing a mask. An enhancer in legal jargon is anything in a criminal act that changes the dynamics of the act for the worse. It increases the amount of time one would face; for instance, without the mask, I faced fifty-five years; with the mask I was facing sixty years in prison.

I walked into the booking room, and the energy I felt let me know how much of a kid I really was. It was daunting and disturbing. I was beyond nervous and no amount of "keepin' it cool" could conceal it. I was booked, made to shower in cold, hard water, and instructed to put some unidentified solution on my head and in my pubic hair that is designed to kill crabs and lice as the deputy stood there and watched to make sure I used it. After I showered, I was given a change of clothes that were a mile too long for me. I had to tie the underwear into a knot on the side to prevent them from falling down while I walked, and the pants as well. When I asked for a smaller size, the deputy, an older, ruddy-looking white guy with what looked to be a permanent scowl, shot back, "You keep what you get!"

I wanted to cry. I kept thinking, *What have I got myself into?*

I was sent upstairs to my pod, which is essentially a housing unit. The one I was sent to was for people with violent crimes who would more than likely get a lot of time. It was bright yellow, smelled stale, and felt desolate in spite of the overpopulation issues that were rampant.

I sat in the county jail for three months. The person I shot and robbed didn't press charges on me, but with my cousin making a statement against me, the state had enough evidence to try and convict me. After all, my cousin did have a direct account of what had taken place that day. There were whispers of me getting probation because I was young, but Judge John Frankie said if I was released without prison time, then it would send the wrong message to future juvenile robbers, as if I pioneered robbery for juveniles.

In turn, at sentencing, after they reduced my charges from attempted homicide to first-degree reckless endangering safety while armed, the robbery count stayed. I received a total of twenty-five years, five for the shooting and twenty for the armed robbery, which was to be served as a stayed sentence after the five was completed. It is called "imposed and stayed." Typically it says that the judge can give you, say, five years' probation and a ten-year imposed and stayed sentence with that, which means if you successfully complete the five years of probation, the ten years vanishes. Suppose you do not successfully make it through, and your probation is revoked. In that case, it means you will be automatically sentenced to ten years in prison because the larger number essentially "eats" the smaller number. Typically, when someone is given an imposed and stayed sentence, the probation sentence is shorter than said imposed and stayed. My twenty-year stayed sentence was parallel to the probation sentence, which at the time was damn near unheard of.

I walked out of court devastated. During every court appearance, I sat there hearing what was being said but not fully comprehending all the legal terms. I asked my lawyer a multitude of questions because I didn't understand what was being said. It was uncanny to me how the judge, district attorney, etc.

were speaking English but they may as well have been speaking Mandarin because I didn't know what was being said. That feeling of ignorance in the presence of people discussing your fate is difficult to shake. I vowed to never experience it again, so I eventually read everything I could get my hands on.

I'd got twenty-five years, and I was fifteen. I couldn't reconcile that in my ninth-grade mind. I came to learn that everyone has a defining moment in their existence where they can say, *my life hasn't been the same since that point*. For some people it's having a child, a promotion at work, maybe relocating to a new city or state, and for others it's an accident or getting in shape etc. For me it was prison.

I served three years and four months of the five years initially; I got out at eighteen, but I had my probation revoked for using a stolen cell phone that belonged to someone I worked with. I received six months for using the phone, which was considered theft of movable property, and seven months and sixteen days revocation. I served in total thirteen months and sixteen days. I came home at twenty with a bitter and angry mentality. I felt myself spiraling out of control mentally. I cut my ankle monitor off, ended up smoking weed again, selling drugs, etc. I was angry at the state, I was angry at my dad, myself—the world.

I stopped caring, which resulted in me having an altercation with six police officers in the summer of 2002. At that time, my initial charges were battery to a police officer, fleeing, and revocation, the latter being an automatic twelve months of incarceration. I wound up doing only the twelve months due to going to court and having the charges reduced and thrown out. I received ninety days for a lesser charge of resisting or obstructing arrest.

I was released on July 24, 2003. On September 25th of that same year for a failed Breathalyzer, I was rearrested and ended up in an unnecessary drug and alcohol abuse treatment program for it. Because I never had a dirty urine analysis or failed Breathalyzer the entire time of my probation and parole, I felt that a drug addiction program for someone without a drug addiction was a waste of time and resources that could have been allocated for something else. It was a three-month program. I completed it without difficulty and was released on February 13, 2004.

I was out for five months before I was arrested again for theft, possession of marijuana, and a trumped-up charge of attempting to disarm a police officer. Six officers drew their guns on me after I fled the arresting officer from where I was living at the time. I had boarded a city bus after the neighborhood was surrounded by squad cars. A Samaritan told that I was on the bus, and before long, they pulled the bus over and boarded with their guns drawn. I put my cell phone down to minimize the possibility of them killing me and saying they thought my phone was a gun.

They ordered me to the ground. I didn't comply. The officer in front of the pack holstered his gun and punched me in my chest. I backed up and blocked his next swing. The rest of them followed suit. I felt fists and feet from every angle. They tried to pull my hands behind my back. On my knees facing one of the seats, I locked my hands together in a fruitless attempt at not being arrested—to no avail. I was taken into custody shortly after that scuffle. I knew I was going to get at least twenty years plus whatever time I had coming for my new charges.

I was revoked for twenty years and was facing fifteen years for all the new charges. With nothing to lose, I was preparing for trial. The day before my trial was scheduled to start, my lawyer came to visit me and told me that the DA would drop every charge if I pled to theft. I agreed and we proceeded from there. I received nine months for theft and ninety days for resisting or obstructing . . . again. The time was being run concurrently, so I had twenty years in total, not twenty-one. I served a total of twelve of the twenty years. Plus the time previously, it has been seventeen years and three months that I've served. I was released at thirty-four on May 3, 2016.

Chapter 2

NEVER STOP, NEVER GIVE UP

I learned over time, as I studied successful people and even the ones considered to be failures, that there are many ways to succeed, yet only one way to fail—and that being to quit. As I sat in prison, every day I searched for reasons to stop pressing on. Well, in the beginning at least, I couldn't fathom what life would be like if I served the entire twenty-year sentence from twenty-two years old. I *wanted* to quit, to end every ounce of sorrow that I was feeling, the self-pity, the self-resentment, the depression. As I searched for reasons to give up on life, all I ever encountered was reasons to persevere.

At about the fourth or fifth-month mark of my twenty years, I was in Dodge Correctional Institution, a maximum-security facility designed to house inmates in the interim period subsequent to sentencing and pre permanent destination. I had gone to the library just to get out my cell for a little while and disrupt my thoughts of going home. The library was an old-looking place that smelled of old book pages,

Bengay, and dampness. It was suspiciously quiet and poorly ventilated but filled with books! Lots of books, a vast variety considering I was in prison.

I walked around aimlessly pretending to look for a book but really just enjoying the "freedom" of roaming. We were able to check out two books at a time, and seeing as how I wasn't *really* there for books, I just grabbed two once the guard instructed us to leave. On the fairly long walk back to my housing unit, I read the synopsis to one of my books, entitled *Kaffir Boy*. Written by a pretty good author named Mark Mathabane, it is the story of a Black boy who was an aspiring tennis player living under the South African apartheid regime. It mainly centers on the vicious brutality of the apartheid system and how he escaped it, and the township Alexandra, to ultimately become a well-known tennis player.

Mathabane also spoke of how Black children and adults dealt with racism and stereotypes, and how he wound up rising above it all. The term *Kaffir* in Afrikaans (from Arabic) is a racial term used to refer to an individual of Nguni ancestry, a group of people who are Zulu, Xhosa, Ndebele, and Swazi who predominantly live in South Africa. The term Kaffir evolved from Cafri, during the precolonial period as an equivalent of Negro. By the mid-twentieth century it was undoubtedly considered an offensive epithet—in short, "nigger."

I immersed myself in the book, turning page after page, finding inspiration on each one. Mark dealt with the worst conditions: hunger, violence, extreme poverty, discrimination, and the eventual hatred and fear of whites. I searched his life for parallels to mine; I compared his situation in the 1980s apartheid era South Africa to my fresh twenty-year sentence in Wisconsin's prison system. There was no comparison. Of course, there were parallels, but my conditions weren't near as extreme as his. I began to feel a little better about my predicament as I read about the raids, the rapes, the murders, the kidnapping, the pillaging of residences, etc., all by the British government's hand which had seized control of South Africa around the early 1800s. It wasn't until 1948 that apartheid, a system of institutionalized racial segregation, was instituted in the country and it lasted until the early 1990s.

The sad part about me having found so much strength and inspiration in *Kaffir Boy* is, I still wasn't emotionally and mentally ready to fully accept my predicament. I relished and wallowed in my own sorrow, tossed and turned at night, and slept less than I'd ever had in my life. Depression was there.

I had stayed two and a half months at Dodge Correctional Institution before I was moved to the county jail, another holding place before I got to where I was going to serve my time. I made it to Oshkosh Correctional Institution on March 22, 2005. I was twenty-three years old and heartbroken. After a couple of months of being there, and seeing too many people I'd known from the streets and other times I was in prison, I started to feel a slight sense of normalcy, although you could tell I was bothered by something.

One particular time I was outside playing basketball, and I was too lax on defense. One of my teammates, a guy a few years older asked me, "What's wrong?"

Now I didn't know this guy from anywhere but the basketball game. So, I'm thinking, *What the fuck you mean, what's wrong?* Out loud I said, "Nothing, why?"

"Yes, it is, I can tell."

I laughed uncomfortably and said, "I'm good."

"Aye, we done, y'all," he told the opposing team as he bounced the ball toward one of them on the opposing team.

"What you doing?" I asked.

"Come walk and talk with me," he responded.

He was absolutely right about something being wrong with me. I had *twenty fucking years!* We walked off the court across the grass in the hot sun to an old rickety picnic table and sat on opposing sides. He looked at me for a few seconds before asking, "How old are you, young dawg?"

"Why?" I responded defensively.

He smirked before responding, "You look like a kid."

"I'm twenty-three." I poked my chest out a little.

"Twenty-three, huh? How much time you got?" he pried.

"Why?" I responded defensively again. "Why you ask so many questions, dawg?" I continued.

"'Cause I can tell somethin' is wrong with you, and I know you just got here, so I figured it must be yo' time structure," he guessed.

Is this nigga a mind reader or some shit? I thought to myself, as I stared at him. "I'm good, man," I told him.

"Go get your P.R.C. papers and I'll go get mine" he said. (P.R.C. = Program Review Committee)

I was hesitant, but I eventually went to get them. We sat back down, and he asked again, "How much time you got?"

I handed him my papers. He looked at them and said, "Aw you only got a dub."

"Only!" I exclaimed. "Nigga, you crazy. They booked the shit outta me, and it's a stated sentence; I'm on revocation!"

"For real?" he asked in disbelief.

"Hell, yea" I said.

"You still good though, lil dawg," he assured me.

I just put my head down. He slid me his papers and said, "Look at this."

I grabbed them and opened them. I looked, and it said, "entry somewhere in 1994," so I looked up at him to search his face for age. I thought he was twenty-something (He was actually thirty). I proceeded to look for his discharge date, and it read, "DECEASED." He'd been locked up nine years on mandatory life sentence for a first-degree intentional homicide that he committed at twenty-one.

I looked at him; he looked back at me.

"You good, lil dawg," he told me again, in a more solemn tone this time.

I averted my eyes out of surprise and a small sense of embarrassment from being so broken and depressed behind my predicament. He went to the "hole" (a segregation unit for discipline in prison) shortly after that conversation, maybe a day or two later, and I'd never seen him again. I think about him and wonder how he's doing from time to time, because he was right, I was going to be okay. I never knew his name, he never knew mine, in spite of us having seen one another's paperwork; it's funny like that in prison sometimes.

For all intents and purposes, I was on a mission to comprise a mental checklist of all the reasons why I shouldn't slit my wrists open and bleed until unconsciousness, or why I shouldn't swan dive head first off the tier I was housed on the moment they unlocked my cell again. You see, because in my mind I had the most gargantuan reason to take my destiny in my own hands and end it all. The survivor in me wouldn't allow it, the warrior in me wouldn't allow it. I wanted to, but I just couldn't.

After years of feeling as if I wanted my life to end, I realized what I really wanted to end was my pain and suffering; my life was okay. I'd gotten a letter from my "brother," one of my closest friends, M&M. He was in prison as well, but in Racine, Wisconsin. He had heard about what happened with me and wrote me to see if I was okay, also to see if what happened was true.

It was. And I had no desire to talk about it.

I was so hurt that I didn't respond to his letter. I knew that he knows who I am, so he didn't take it personally. He wound up there with me later, so I was able to apologize in person before I was released. He told me there was no need to because he understood what I must have been going through mentally. That's my brother till this day.

I also met another one of my good friends whom I consider a brother. His name is Quan. At the time he had five years and was scheduled to be released on December 8, 2009. We talked and formulated plans over the next four and a half years on a regular basis.

I had written five urban novels (none of them published) after I'd read *Let That Be the Reason* by Vickie Stringer, who is now the publisher of Triple Crown Publications. I was a rapper, not an author, but I'd read an article in the November-December 2004 issue of *King Magazine*, with Christina Milian on the cover, that detailed Vickie Stringer's journey from federal prison to successful author and publishing company owner. I figured since I couldn't do much in music, I might as well start writing books. I started with really short stories for my cellmate to read and critique. Things progressed from there.

Quan and I came up with a plan: We would start a publishing company. I had written the books, first one being *Sex, Money, and Murder,* and named him as coauthor to ensure his portion of the proceeds. Needless to say, we never published it or its follow-up, *Redemption,* or the three that came after them. My mind had gone to so many different places within the two years that I'd written those five books that I completely lost interest in the urban fiction genre altogether. I was still searching, inspired by so many stories of people's predicaments and lives, but I still wasn't 100 percent convinced of the quality in my own self-worth and what I truly had to offer the world.

I was one test away from completing my high school equivalent diploma(HSED) in 2006. I was a few months away from turning twenty-five and focusing really hard on getting a passing grade because that was all I needed. I scored so high on all the other tests that I had taken during my previous prison stays that I didn't have to do much in math. Needless to say, I passed, but I missed the quarterly graduation ceremony because I had a fight with an annoying white guy that nobody liked.

My mom came to see me when I was in the hole. She asked me what happened as we spoke through the dense, cold glass of the segregation visiting area. I looked in her eyes and couldn't bring myself to say, *I was in his room to beat him up after he butted in a conversation that Quan and I were having without saying excuse me. . .* So what I said, knowing that my mom is a Black woman filled with racial pride and cultural affinity with zero tolerance for racism or discrimination, was" He called me a nigger."

Her response, "Well, you should have kicked his ass, then."

I showed her my test results, which I received in the mail since I'd been in the hole, which diverted her attention from my current predicament to a more positive one. My mother always stressed the importance of education and literacy. Her favorite thing to tell me as a kid was "Don't no woman want no dumb man!" At eleven or twelve I used to think, *What the hell is she talking about?* She would give me one of her textbooks—she was in school for liberal arts—and tell me to read a chapter, look up every word that I didn't know, write it down, use it in a sentence, and then come and tell her what I just read. I hated it at the time, but it became a thing I did that I grew to love. I was also thinking, *This is cruel. She knows I hate it and she still makes me do it.*

The first thing she said to me after I went to prison was, "You better read. Don't just sit around playing games and shit." That became one of my mantras for life, so now when I have what I would typically consider free time, I use it to do something constructive that will add to me.

I knew that when I showed my mom my test results that day in the hole, she would be proud and happy for me. The conversation that followed her knowing I was now a high school graduate was ethereal and pleasant until we were told that our time was up. She was initially saddened and concerned by the fact that I was visibly ten or fifteen pounds lighter than the last time she saw me, due to the food portions in segregation being so small, but she eventually moved past that once the education talk started, and we had a great visit until it was time to go. Many other times my mom and I had difficulty parting ways until the next time, but with my accomplishment, this time was filled with hope and possibilities. We shared a smile through that glass, exchanged I love you's and said, "I'll see you later."

Even with all the positive things that I was working toward, and those that I'd already accomplished, I still was having difficulty accepting twenty years. I couldn't say it. The odd thing was that the year I'd gotten revoked, the number twenty seemed to have a lot of symbolism. Prince had done interviews on numerous media outlets for the twentieth anniversary of his acting debut and album of the same name, *Purple Reign.* The twentieth anniversary of the first *Terminator* movie was all over entertainment shows. My girlfriend at the time turned twenty. That number seemed to be all around me, yet I couldn't say it because if I did, it made the length of my sentence *real* in my mind.

My uncle was there with me also. He was a lifer who had been away since 1988, seventeen years at the time, for a homicide he'd committed when I was six years old. I hadn't seen him since that time, and it was nothing short of surreal to see him now that I was an adult. He'd heard about all my antics in the streets and thought that I would come to where he was with the same behavior and (in prison terminology), "fuck off his bid." Little did he know that was the furthest thing from my mind. I was just trying to process it all. We walked the track for hours on end, getting to know each other not only as people but as men. I told him how life was on the streets, how so many things had changed since he was away, and he told me how life had been for him in prison all those years, period.

One of the most important things that he ever told me was "Don't ever look back, nephew; you gotta keep your eyes ahead. Only look back to reflect and check your progress, and leave the street on the street." I didn't fully understand the latter part of his statement at the time, but I did eventually. I had to keep myself from being too concerned with what was going on in society, and the street, in order to keep my head together while I was there. He also made it a point to tell me, "Always do you, nephew. Make sure you put yourself in a position to see to it that you do good."

We would talk for hours, laugh, joke, and reminisce in an attempt to invoke some kind of normalcy into our predicament. One day someone knocked on my door and told me, "Your uncle want you outside." I knew it had to be something because it was October and not many people were outside because of the chill that was in the air.

I saw him on the track standing in one spot waiting for me. I walked up and said, "What's up, unc?"

He looked at me with tears in his eyes and handed me an obituary clipping from the newspaper. It was my aunt, the mother of two of his kids. She had passed away from lymphoma. It was the first and only time I saw my uncle cry. I didn't know what to do, so I just hugged him and held him as tightly as I could. He hugged me back after a brief hesitation. And then we started walking, and I listened to all the stories he had about "Dimples" (her nickname) as he reminisced. The most interesting thing about that moment for me was the unexpected vulnerability from someone I saw in a completely different light, yet whom I admire. Prison shaped and molded a friendship between my uncle and me, a camaraderie that was much deeper than the typical uncle - nephew acquaintance. It remains to this day.

I continued on my quest for reasons to continue living this hellish existence: the daily attempts of dehumanization by correctional officers, the sleepless nights, the dreams of being free only to awake to sheer disappointment from the realization of still being trapped, the rampant homosexuality, and the pedophiles. Then there was the distorted thinking of the guys who swore they weren't gay because according to them, "I only got my *dick* sucked" or "He ain't *fuckin'* me." My uncle used to say, "If you flip, you'll flop" or "If you'll pitch, you'll hit." In other words, it is a two-way street in what we deemed to be illicit behavior.

I searched for reasons and stumbled upon *Up from Slavery*, the 1901 autobiography of Booker T. Washington. In it he describes his personal experience of having worked his way from being a child slave during the Civil War through every obstacle he faced and vanquished to get an education at Hampton Normal and Agricultural Institute (now Hampton University). A portion of his philosophy was diligence and education, something I had heard a million times from my mom. A few major themes in the book were:

- what it means to be your own person
- industriousness
- humility
- the people's capacity for personal evolution
- poverty among the Black population

Up from Slavery was a nonconfrontational message of self-sufficiency and self-actualization that was careful not to rub the wrong people—white fascist Southerners—the wrong way at a time when, according to them, *Blacks* and *education* was oxymoronic. To sum up a man of great prestige and courage, Booker T. was an accommodationist (which explains why W.E.B. Du Bois believed that he failed in his sensitivity to African Americans. In his seminal work, *The Souls of Black Folk*, Du Bois, with his Niagara Movement, established himself in opposition to Booker T.'s conciliatory existence.)

One of the most popular quotes by Booker T. is his hand metaphor that was made in his Atlanta exposition speech on October 18, 1895: "In all things that are purely social we can be as separate as the fingers, yet one as the hand in all things essential to mutual progress" (Washington, 1895). In short, we do not need to "hang" with you, but we might need you from time to time. I studied Booker T. and W.E.B. Du Bois and drew lots of inspiration from both of those brilliant men. How could someone (Booker T. Washington), born a slave, be filled with so much drive and ambition to succeed that he becomes an educator, builds an institution for education from the ground up, and goes on to become one of the greatest orators of the nineteenth century? No matter how much of his philosophy I (or whomever else) disagree with, that alone was enough for me to find something else to live for. I was not born a slave. I was in prison—slavery by another name, of course—but I wasn't born there, so to end my life after knowing his story would be nothing short of disservice to Booker T. Washington's legacy.

William Edward Burghardt Du Bois, born February 23, 1868, was a sociologist, socialist, historian, civil rights activist, author, and many other meritorious things. Born in Great Barrington, Massachusetts, he was the first African American to earn a doctorate from Harvard, having done undergraduate work at the University of Berlin. Then he went on to become a professor of history, sociology, and economics at Atlanta University. He was also one of the founders of the NAACP, along with Moorfield Storey, Ida B. Wells-Barnett and Mary White Ovington in 1909, which was preceded by his leadership of the Niagara Movement, a group of African American activists that pushed equality for Blacks.

The Niagara Movement completely opposed the Atlanta Compromise, which ultimately said that Blacks would remain in a perceived subordinate position until "hard work" would pay off and we somehow would become "equal" to whites. Instead, the Niagara Movement took a more radical stance: "Through helplessness we may submit, but the voice of protest of ten million Americans must never cease to assail the ears of their fellows so long as America is unjust" (*Niagara Declaration*, 1905).

Du Bois insisted on full rights, increased political representation and participation, which he believed would be brought about by a group that he dubbed the

Talented Tenth (Du Bois, 1903). The concept of "racial uplift" was designed to increase the chances for advanced education of African Americans to develop. In his collection of essays, *The Souls of Black Folks*, Du Bois uses the term *color line* borrowed from Fredrick Douglass (1881), "The problem with the twentieth century is the problem of the color line" (Du Bois, 1903). Du Bois believed that capitalism was a primary cause of racism and he was generally sympathetic to socialist causes throughout his life.

As I studied Du Bois and realized the tension that existed between him and Booker T., it didn't matter to me. All that mattered was how they both inspired me, along with Nelson Mandela, to preserve and keep the faith—whatever that faith was. After reading Mandela's autobiography, *Long Walk to Freedom*, I figured if Nelson Mandela could maintain and retain his sanity through twenty-seven years of a life sentence, eighteen of those years spent on Robben Island, west of Cape Town, South Africa, in an eight-foot-by-seven-foot concrete cell with only a straw mat to sleep on, and yet rise to become the president of his country. Then I can weather a twenty-year storm and become whatever—a president, an astronaut, a cosmonaut, a cosmetologist—absolutely anything.

I chose to embark on a journey of extreme self-improvement. I started with the completion of my high school diploma. As I stated before, I had one test left to achieve that: math. I enrolled in school and passed on the first attempt, unlike many others I had witnessed. I was twenty-five. After that, feeling inspired and unstoppable, I saw an advertisement for a Microsoft Office program and remembered that I had read in *Psychology Today* magazine that six months out of society is equal to being two years behind in technology. At the time I'd been away for almost four years which meant that I was nearly sixteen years behind on technology, so I figured the least I could do was gain some degree of computer literacy.

So, I enrolled in the Microsoft Office course through Fox Valley Technical College in Appleton, Wisconsin, near Oshkosh. I passed with flying colors. I even opted to take the electives and received my certificate with the rest of the graduates. I felt great. I attended my very first graduation ever. I had gotten expelled from school, so I was unable to walk across the stage in junior high. Then, I never completed the ninth grade, so there was obviously no high school graduation. I was in segregation when I received my HSED, so I missed that ceremony as well. But I made the Microsoft Office festivities. My mom and stepdad came to support me as they always did, and the day went off without a hitch.

The ironic thing about those achievements at that time is that I knew within that I wasn't fully ready to embrace change or happiness. I allowed myself to find comfort in a dystopian state. Given the predicament, I found it easy to be downtrodden and sad. In the backdrop of my sense of humor and joviality existed this dark cloud that helped me write great songs and was the impetus for me exercising excessively until I had nearly zero percent body fat. I started after I had got word my younger cousin was killed by a stray bullet at a house party; she was twenty-five. Forty-two miles a week I ran in an attempt to clear my head. It worked, but I was losing weight rapidly.

I eventually stopped running, and I wound up sinking into myself as I dwelled on the fact that I was twenty-six and serving twenty years for a crime I committed when I was fifteen years old, the fact that the state waived my case into adult court, the fact that I had gotten revoked for twenty years for violation of probation because of a misdemeanor. My outlet was writing. I did it relentlessly at a frantic pace. When that became boring, I worked out. When *that* stopped working, I read; then I repeated the rotation. I lived in my head all the time and allowed my existence to be guided by the dreams I had for my life. I wanted to be successful, to be admired, to be respected, to be liked, loved and heard, etc.

Most of all I wanted to be *free.* That for me was the be-all and end-all. *Free.* I repeated that to myself daily I looked up the definition and studied it.

free (Fre), adj.,

1) enjoying personal rights or liberty, as one who is not in slavery or confinement.
2) pertaining to or reserved for those who enjoy personal liberty.
3) possessing political liberties
4) enjoying political independence, as a people or a country not under foreign rule.
5) exempt from external authority, interference, or restriction, independent, free choice. (Webster's, 2001)

It was definition number five that made me feel as if it was attainable; to be exempt from external authority was my new goal. I decided to go from cornrows to dreads because to be exempt from external authority regarding hair, to me, meant no barbershop. By "freeing" my mind I read *everything,* mainly biographies and nonfiction. I embarked on a quest to acquire all the things via information that could never be taken from me.

I felt trapped physically, but I knew that I could go anywhere I wanted mentally. I knew that they couldn't prevent me from dreaming, from hoping or wishing. All this existed within me, next to my looming depression and frustration from having no one else to blame for my predicament but myself. The notion that life was passing me by on the outside world gnawed at me mentally day in and day out. I faked being okay when I was on the phone with my parents or when they came to see me because I knew they came to see the person they missed, not the cynical, overly analytical, depressed, hate-filled, militant-minded person I had become.

I studied every Black Panther biography from *Soul on Ice* by Eldridge Cleaver to *Soledad Brother: The Prison Letters of George Jackson*. I was fascinated by the stories of Angela Davis and Assata Shakur. I studied the system, specifically the American justice system, and the more I learned, the angrier I became bitter even. I became obsessed with historical occurrences regarding race relations in America and how Blacks always seemed to come up with the short end of the stick, from the Black Codes to the destruction of Black Wall Street, from the civil rights movement to our civil rights being in constant violation. I delved into the story of Emmett Till, much deeper than school would have ever been willing to teach me, and how Carolyn Bryant Donham (wife of Roy Bryant) fabricated a story that lead to Emmett Till's murder.

I read the lives of Nat Turner, Bob Johnson, Napoleon Hill, Marcus Garvey, Ella Baker, Josephine Baker, Adolf Hitler, Adolf and Rudolf Dassler, etc. I studied Karl Marx, Mao Zedong, Carl Jung, George Jung, and a host of others. You name it, I read it. I examined their lives so deeply that they became my peers and teachers. Plato taught me his dialogues; I learned of Seneca's tragedies, Aristotle's school, the lyceum, and how he rejected Plato's theory of forms, which is the notion that the physical world is not as real or true as timeless unchangeable ideas. I learned more about Tookie Williams and how California's governor at the time, Arnold Schwarzenegger, refused to grant clemency from his execution in spite of Williams having changed his life amid authoring nine anti-gang books for teens. I learned more about Charles S. Dutton, famous for his role as a noble garbage man on the TV series *Roc*, and how he served seven and a half years for manslaughter before changing his life and becoming a successful award-winning actor. I read about Bernard Hopkins, the former middle and lightweight boxing champion, who served nearly five years in prison of an eighteen-year sentence for nine felonies and was released in 1988 and won his first title fight in 1995 with a victory over Steve Frank by way of technical knockout which, he stopped in twenty-four seconds. He went on to successfully defend his title seventeen times and in 2011 and became the oldest man in history to win a major world title at forty-six years old.

I read about famed actor Danny Trejo, best known for his convincing roles in *From Dusk till Dawn* and *Desperado* and, He served eleven years in San Quentin State Prison in California for trying to pass sugar as cocaine to an undercover agent. After he decided to turn his life around, Trejo became a drug counselor. Someone that he was mentoring worked with a movie crew. Trejo visited him on set, was noticed by the casting director, and made it into the movie as an extra.

I purposely sought out stories of redemption because they were drenched in inspiration, specifically redemption stories about people coming from prison and doing great things. I figured, *If they could climb out of this hopeless abyss of despair, cynicism, dehumanization, degradation, confinement and strife, then why can't I? Why can't I find beauty in my greatest struggle?* As much as I wanted to quit, I knew quitting was the only way to fail. I felt like if heaven or hell is real and our souls will eternally live in one of those two places in the afterlife, then how would I explain to Malcolm, Martin, Marcus, Emmet, Harriett, Pac, Fred Hampton, Mark Clark, and all my other heroes that I admire?

Admiring them, I simply couldn't take an ordeal that was significantly less threatening to me than what they'd lived through and lost their lives in the midst of. I was going to eliminate my suffering by *suicide*? Something didn't sit right with me when I thought about it deeply. I started to feel selfish, like I was trying to cheat or shortcut to greatness. No cheat code, some of us get there faster than others, but there is always the process. There is a beaten track and there is a route that is off the beaten track. I remember as a kid I used to love walking on undisturbed snow; it was more exciting and exhilarating. Also, the idea of me being the first one to not only walk but create this path in the snow was so fulfilling. The trampled snow, the beaten track, was less appealing although it was easier because people had gone that way already. So I felt I had to keep going no matter how hard it became. No matter how bleak it looked, I was determined, and as the song "Courage Under Fire" says, "Never stop, never give up, I don't care what you face if you fall make sure you get up."

What we do is what we choose, I chose to fight, strive, thrive, and ultimately *win*.

Chapter 3

WORK ON YOU

Everything begins and ends with you. I don't recall exactly where I heard it, or who I heard say it; all I know is that it resonated with me deeply. It echoed within my mind like a much-needed compliment on a bad hair day.

It was 2010, I was creeping up on six years in prison and probably my fourth year of stockpiling reasons not to give up. The news outlets were doing hourly reports on the magnitude 7.0 earthquake that shook the town of Leogane in Haiti, leaving a reported two hundred thousand people dead on January 12. I couldn't believe how much damage it caused, how many lives were taken, and how much I still found myself complaining about my predicament with things like that going on in the world. My heart truly went out to the people of Haiti, and I silently asked for forgiveness for being so blinded by my struggles.

It was due to Haiti's predicament and my own that I felt the need to write something. That something wound up being a song that shares its title with this book. I still needed something else to impel me to carry on. The irony of it was that once I finished writing the song, I realized that every encouraging word, every nudge I needed, every positive word I needed to hear was already within me. I was blown away by the words I put on paper that came from my heart. I memorized that song as quickly as possible, along with the poem "Invictus" by William E. Henley. I recited them both to myself on a daily basis, whenever I fell down, whenever my spirits were up. I rapped it to everybody and told everybody I socialized with regularly about "Invictus." I felt the confidence in the "new" me growing exponentially every day, and I loved how it felt.

It was also around this time that one of my homeboys, Jeremy, typically known as Diamond, suggested I read a book that he had, *How to Hustle and Win: A Survival Guide for the Ghetto* by a guy named Supreme Understanding. His name alone intrigued me, so I took it back to my cell and began reading right away. The foreword is by a well-known former drug kingpin, Freeway Ricky Ross, whose story I was all too familiar with and who was someone else I'd admired because through hard work, research and self-belief, he'd gotten his life sentence commuted to a twenty-year sentence. He served thirteen years and was released in 2009. In his foreword he stated, "An ounce of prevention is better than a pound of care." I immediately wrote it down in my memo pad because it made so much more sense to me.

How to Hustle and Win changed my perspective on so many things. It ran the gamut of topics from how to beat a criminal charge to Che Guevara, from street hustling skills to corporate assertions, from the illusions of the American Dream for Blacks to the false notion of the superiority of whites, from COINTELPRO to Stevie Williams, from the Nation of Gods and Earths to the wrong foods to eat. In *How to Hustle and Win* there was an illustration of a mirror; on the mirror it read, "You are now looking at the cause of all your problems." That shit slapped me in the face, and it coincided with "Everything begins and ends with you."

I put the book down momentarily and put a question mark on *everything* that I had blamed other people for. All the *you* statements or *them* statements, all the *He did this* or *She did that* or *They made me mad.* I worked on accepting what *they* did while controlling how I responded to what *they* did. I'd written myself a ten-point program to help myself react more effectively to people, not only in prison, but in life.

1. You can't control other people's emotions, only how you react to them.

2. Most of the time how people feel has nothing to do with you at all; you just happen to be in front of them.

3. Your reputation lies in the minds of other people; you can do whatever, they will draw their own conclusion.

4. You cannot control what people think about, but you can influence it by action.

5. One person's opinion of you is just that.

6. They don't believe that you can do it, because they don't believe that *they* can do it.

7. If they are negative toward you, imagine how they are to themselves.

8. If they get angry quickly, it just means that they are sensitive, and the toughness is likely a façade, or defense mechanism.

9. If they hold themselves to a higher standard, they will hold you to a higher one as well.

10. If they will not accept change, *run*.

11. That list was written more than a decade ago. I read it daily because I chose to become the kind of person that I admired.

I learned that to be and do anything worthwhile in life you have to take a long, hard, honest look at yourself. I did just that. One day I sat at the desk in my cell with my pen and writing pad in front of me. I began to write my strengths; on the other side was my weaknesses. I chose twelve and twelve, reason being is because twelve represents the completion of a cycle, and typically thirteen signifies transitions (e.g., twelve months in a year. It is also said to represent divinity, perfection, harmony, achievement, etc.). So, I chose twelve for each one.

THIS IS MY LIST:

Strengths	Weaknesses
1. Ambitious	1. Impulsive
2. Extroverted	2. Loquacious
3. Articulate	3. Too trusting
4. Analytical	4. Know-it-all
5. Talented	5. Too sensitive
6. Humorous	6. Impatient with others
7. Realistically Optimistic	7. High expectations of others
8. Confident	8. Stubborn
9. Self-Reliant	9. Extremely opinionated
10. Intelligent	10. Can be passive aggressive
11. Compassionate	11. Too forgiving
12. A dreamer	12. A dreamer

I recommend everybody to take a moment to take a hard look at themselves to figure out what their strengths and weaknesses are. Write them down in order to look at them and map out a plan to turn those weaknesses into strengths. That was my first list, written on January 1, 2013. The following is my newer one.

MY 2020 LIST:

Strengths

1. Goal oriented
2. Understanding
3. Purpose driven
4. Teachable
5. Patient
6. Self-aware
7. Discipline
8. Assertive
9. Outspoken
10. Resilient
11. Extroverted
12. Lover of people

Weaknesses

1. Want more for others, than they want for themselves
2. Impulsive
3. At times I only seek the good in people
4. Overly opinionated
5. A huge emphasis on logic/ not enough emotion
6. Stubborn
7. Dweller (on mental things)
8. Impatient with people
9. Too detached from emotion at times
10. Can be passive aggressive
11. Can be overly aggressive
12. I don't let things go as I should

As you can see the 2020 list slightly differs from the first list, which ultimately shows growth and greater self-awareness. This exercise heightened my self-awareness and led to an honest reflection of who I really am and also who I wanted to become. In my mind, having been away for nearly seven years, I wholeheartedly believed that I was behind the curve on all things. Not just technology, all things academically, socially, musically, etc. So what I did was I bought books on every subject and I studied the new guys who came into prison. I became even more of a sponge than I was when I was growing up looking up to my uncles, older cousins and their friends. I refused to let the world pass me by. I studied every reference book from *The New York Times Guide to Essential Knowledge* to annual almanacs, which led me to something that I like to call The Mirror Theory or TMR. The Mirror Theory is rooted on five principles:

> Self-Love
> Self-Respect
> Self-Belief
> Self-Actualization
> Self-Reliance

Self-Love

Self-love seems like a pretty simple concept at first glance and it is for the most part. The complexity comes in when we realize that a lot of us were never really taught to love ourselves the way that we were taught to love others. Love mom and dad, grandparent, siblings, friends, etc. A lot of us learn to love ourselves by trial and error after putting ourselves in harm's way via an unhealthy relationship or a potentially dangerous situation. Often we are instructed to focus on our outer appearance, hairdos, clean clothes, good hygiene, etc. While all those are good things to get into the habit of maintaining, they mean less than our inner appearance, a good character, wholesome principles, necessary values, our intellect, etc.

Assata Shakur once said, "Our consciousness creates what comes out of our mouths, and what comes out of our mouths reflects our consciousness" (Marable, 1997). So, through self-love I focused more on the inner me, how I spoke to people (in my tone, word choice, delivery, etc.),what I read, who I spent my time with, and how I spent my time with that person or those people.

Once you begin to love yourself properly you won't be so quick to give your most precious commodity, time, to those you feel don't deserve it. In short, love yourself as much as you were taught to love other people.

Self-Respect

Self-respect is profoundly important because in its absence, respect is unable to be received. Dignity within teaches others how to treat you, and it shows that you know and understand your worth. There are five easy ways to show and detect self-respect:

1. Respect others
2. Make good choices
3. Know that people deserve to be forgiven just as you desire to be forgiven
4. Never talk down to yourself. Be honest and turn weaknesses into strengths but never talk down to yourself.
5. Don't violate your own moral code. In other words, hold yourself to a particular standard and never allow anyone to deceive you into violating that.

Self-Belief

I remember being in high school, going to basketball tryouts with a good friend of mine. He was the best player that I had ever seen at the time. He knew he was good. He was brash and arrogant on the playground, even at the Boys & Girls Club while playing. He was quick, had a "wet" jump shot, as we call it (a good jump shot), a deadly crossover, and athleticism to marvel at. When it came to basketball tryouts, though, he was surprisingly hesitant. I encouraged him as much as I could, but he refused to even leave the bleachers with me. I was shocked. We watched as another boy who was ten times less skilled than my friend not only try out but make the team because he had a belief in himself that was undeniable. Nearly palpable.

I eventually learned that the ones who succeed in life are not the most qualified or the most talented, but they are the ones who believe in themselves and the ones who outwork everyone. Sometimes that first step toward somethings is the most daunting and intimidating, but the next fifty come with confidence and conviction. All you must do is possess this little thing called self-belief.

Self-Actualization

Self-actualization simply means to achieve your full potential through creativity, independence, spontaneity, and a grasp of the real world.

I met a good friend in 2006 while I was in prison. He had forty years and had been away for ten when we met. I was twenty-four on the verge of being twenty-five; he had just turned thirty-four. I first took notice of his energy as we sat in the dayroom that was filled with idle chatter and the occasional Sit down! from an overzealous corrections officer. My soon-to-be "homeboy" seemed to carry himself with confidence and positive energy. He even had a bounce in his step that made me think he may have been close to release.

We eventually met officially on the basketball court and hit it off. He sort of became like a big brother to me. Over the next eight years of our time in prison, we had countless thought-provoking conversations, walked hundreds of laps on the outside track, exchanged ideas, traded books, played countless games of basketball (he's better, by the way), worked out, debated, etc. He was also my barber in there (sometimes out here as well). I was released in May 2016; he was released in October of the same year. After his release he bought a barbershop and named it Hair Code, the concept being that what was once the street code is now the hair code. He also owns a trucking company, is an author of an amazing piece of literature entitled "The Answers," and is a highly sought after motivational "doer" (not speaker) as he describes it, along with countless other endeavors. My friend Ed Hennings, after serving twenty years in prison, is the definition of self-actualization.

What we must do is do more than we speak, act more than we think, and place strategy before execution. Ed's twenty years were the strategic portion of his life's journey, and he allowed them to greatly prepare him for the execution. Nothing is stopping you from being whatever it is that you desire to be. Henry

Ford said it best, "Whether you believe you can, or believe you can't; you're right."

Self-Reliance

In 1841, Ralph Waldo Emerson published a phenomenal essay on self-reliance that struck a chord with me when I read it for the first time around 2008. Emerson details "the need for each individual to avoid conformity and false consistency, and follow his own instincts and ideas" Wikipedia, 2020). One of his most famous quotes is "A foolish consistency is the hobgoblin of little minds, adored by little statesmen and philosophers and divines" (Emerson, 1841). In other words, foolish consistency causes unnecessary superstitions and is only admired by the small and narrow-minded.

I named the fifth principle of TMT Self-Reliance because it is a solid foundation for the previous four. When we rely on ourselves, the important, often overlooked aspects of who we are, then we will not have a desire for outside validation, nor will we have a need. In a lot of cases we find ourselves in pursuit of happiness that we refuse to see in the mirror, and we deceive ourselves into thinking that someone else has the power to make us happy. Well, I'll tell you something: If they have the power to make you happy, then you have given them the power to make you unhappy. All the positives within us can only be supplemented by the pleasantries of someone else. I don't mean self-reliance in the sense of not ever needing external assistance, but self-reliance in the sense of knowing your worth and knowing that the value of your worth is astronomically high. You just have to see it and lead with it.

The "Hustla" in You

We each have in us a desire to be something that we consider greater than who we are at the moment. When I was in prison I knew that my predicament wasn't for me. I knew that I was only passing through, no matter how many times I passed through because my probation had been revoked or because I'd foolishly committed another crime. I knew that it was simply a level in my life that I was passing in order to get to something greater. Right now, you might be on a level in your life that you dislike. It may be financial. It might be social. You might even have a less than ideal living situation. You may be in a relationship that seems less than fulfilling. You may even be in prison, jobless, or homeless. None of that truly matters. What truly matters is the fact that you have the power to make it all change or make a change within your current situation. That thing that drives the desire to be better and have better is what I call the hustla (hustler) in *you*.

Ahead are my four steps to fully actualize that hustler that lives in us all:

1. Down is not out.
2. Expand or be expendable.
3. Pursue mastery over money.
4. Think big but start small.

It was a Monday night, April 1, 2019, when the Los Angeles Clippers were playing the Golden State Warriors in game two of the first round of the playoffs. Being down one game in the series, the Clippers were looking to even it at a game apiece. And that they did, in historic fashion. Golden State led by as much as thirty-one points with the score being ninety-four, sixty-three by the middle of the third quarter. The Clippers refused to believe that they were out, even though they were clearly down by what seemed to be an insurmountable deficit.

Led by shooting guard Lou Williams's thirty-six points and eleven assists (with the help of twenty-two turnovers by the Warriors, nine by Kevin Durant) and Montrezl Harrell's double-double of twenty-five points and ten boards (rebounds), the Clippers made an impressive thirty-one, fourteen run to cut the

Warriors lead to fourteen. They never let up, and with just 16.5 seconds left on the clock, Landry Shamet gave the Clippers a 133 to 131 lead. Harrell helped them cap the game off with two free throws that made it 135 to 131, making that victory the biggest in NBA Playoff history. While the Clippers didn't win the series against the defending champs, they showed a resilience that was unmatched and earned a well-deserved level of respect from those who weren't even Clippers fans.

I was facing sixty years in prison at fifteen years old. I received twenty-five; I served seventeen years total, but twelve of those years straight. I knew all along that I would be okay, because I believed in me. Sometimes we must endure extreme hardships and bump our heads several times before we get it. I eventually got it; for one, I chose to, and second, I never stopped believing. I knew that just because I was down, I was not out, and neither are you. In the words of one of my favorite rock groups, Journey, "Don't Stop Believin'."

A large part of life is about providing a quality service that people will compensate you financially for. Money should never be the goal. It is the result of accomplishing the goal; it can also be used to accomplish the goal. Yet it is expendable, replaceable, and the interesting thing is that we trade our time for it, but we cannot do it in reverse. There is no logic in giving the least replaceable thing (time) for the most replaceable (money). So when I say pursue mastery over money, it is mastery of all things necessary: mastery of self, mastery of skill, etc. If you rap, then you should read and write a lot in order to sharpen your skills. Work on delivery, conviction in your speech, cadence, inflection, and to better understand language and rhetoric. Whatever it is that you do, surround yourself with likeminded people so that you can remain in that head space and always feel that specific energy that will encourage and not discourage.

Embody the goal. Walk in it. You must be who you want to be in your head before you can ever be it externally. So, harness the greatness that already exists within you. Don't worry too much about the money because *it* arrives the moment that you do.

Russell Simmons

I fell in love with hip-hop as very young child. It was so exciting to be able to see people on TV who looked like me, telling stories that I could not only relate to but that I've lived. The first movie that captured my attention regarding hip-hop was the story of Russell Simmons and Rick Rubin and the beginning of Def Jam records, Krush Groove. I was four years old. For me, as an artist myself, the movie details the fire inside that is needed to effectively pursue a goal. For them that goal was getting the record label off the ground. Russell "Rush" Simmons would not only get the label off the ground with Rick Rubin, he went on to become what we know today as one of the godfathers of hip-hop.

He used the same drive and determination that it took to start and complete that venture, to start and successfully run Phat Farm clothing, Rush Management, Def Comedy Jam, Def Poetry Jam, and a host of other ventures.

During my time in confinement, I said to myself, If Russell could, then why can't I? I focused on the willpower it took to step out on faith in order to live the life that I not only want but that I deserve as well. Once I decided that I'd had enough of prison, I thought about all the no's that he and Rick heard before they chose to take their destiny into their own hands. I'd heard no from the parole board so often that I conditioned myself mentally to complete my entire sentence while at the same time preparing myself for life after my release because I knew it was coming.

One of my favorite quotes by Russell Simmons that I live by is "Be encouraged. Stay on your hustle. You can't fail unless you quit." I repeated that in my head a thousand times over until it became second nature. That's what you have to do to be a better version of yourself: Immerse yourself in the betterment of yourself so that you can accomplish anything you set out to do. Things seem so impossible until you start the process and begin to see progress, even if it's a change in your mentality.

Rush once said, "Do you!" I did me. Now I encourage you to do the same, no matter where you are in life. If you want more or better, then forget the no's that you may hear that cause hesitance, because the ones around you don't matter. Keep going, keep pushing, and always keep your fire.

Chapter 4:

ALWAYS FOLLOW THROUGH

I learned early on that finishing what you start (always following through) strengthens discipline and creates a focus that can positively affect other areas of your life. My mother used to tell me, "Don't start what you can't finish," I've carried that with me my entire life and when I was in prison with that 20 years it led me to something that I like to call "The Simpatico Effect," which I wrote a four point plan to highlight and emphasize the effect and how it should be applied.

1. Hang with those who inspire you, not compete with you.
2. Hang with those who are working toward something positively life-changing.
3. Hang with those who hold you accountable.
4. Hang with those who won't let you quit

When I was a kid my uncle use to always tell me, "If you hang with nine broke people you'll be the tenth one." Translation, if you have goals you can't expect to get to where you need to be in life by hanging with people who are content with where they are, I'm pretty sure you've heard the idiom, "birds of a feather flock together." We are all fallible people and we are here to serve different purposes in one another's lives. Darryl "white folks" Woodson said it perfectly in his analogy of ducks and geese. "You never see ducks hang with geese even though they are both water fowl." With that I'll detail how the Simpatico Effect works.

People who inspire us are typically those who are doing better than us at the moment, or those who are working toward something greater than themselves. That normally inspires you to want to do something greater than what you've been doing and work toward something that can/will inspire others. On the other end of the spectrum are the actions, or lack thereof, that evoke inspiration. For me personally when I see someone who seems not to want much out of life, it inspires me to do more so as not to end up like that person, so the outcome is inspiration on both ends; but the source of it is vastly different. The inertia in some people makes me want to "get to it" (success) and the total opposite makes me want to get to it, either way I'm getting to it.

Hang with Those Who Inspire You, Not Compete with You

You will notice those "friends" who view you as competition seem to always make negative comments in a joking manner. If you like a particular woman and your friend jokingly says, "She won't mess with you," it's more than likely because he secretly doesn't want her to mess with you. Maybe he wants her for himself. Also, if your friend tries to discourage you from pursuing what you love and believe in, it's probably because they lack something to pursue, or they lack self-belief, so they would rather see you stay on their level than to watch you soar. In the street, those are called haters; some people call them "frenemies." They may be called something else the world over, but it all means the same thing: They want to compete, not inspire.

When I came home from prison, one of the first things that really stood out to me was that a lot of people that I'd known before I went away were still doing the same thing—and not on a larger scale. It was as if they'd been static and stagnant for twelve years, not all of them, but many of them. I was disappointed because while I was away, in my mind, everyone was taking advantage of all the opportunities that I would have had at my fingertips had I been physically free. When I was released I couldn't believe the lack of growth that existed in people I once admired and those I had once considered friends. I found myself upset with them at times because I had just endured what I considered to be my lowest point in life. There are not many tangible and viable options presented to you in prison. That's not to imply that they are *presented* to you in the "free" world, but there is nothing but *you* preventing you from getting to those options and opportunities.

So when I was released, I realized that I'd only been held captive physically. My mind was never captured or content. Also, my physical confinement was by force. Though it was due to a choice that I made, if I could have chosen not to go to prison, believe me I would have. So as I sat in the presence of people I couldn't wait to see, I found myself feeling out of place and pretending to be who I once was. Not because they were simply used to that version of me but because they hadn't grown far beyond that version of themselves, the old me was who they identified with.

I've always understood that growing old is mandatory while growing up is optional, and some people simply choose not to grow up. Some never want anything out of life other than what they already have or think they know. I wasn't willing to settle for the old me. I had been inspired in prison by reading about people who competed against nobody but channeled their energy into more positive achievements. Now that I was out of prison, I made the choice to hang with people who inspired me instead of those who competed or settled.

Hang with Those Who Are Working toward Something Positively Life-Changing

When I was in prison, after so long of course, I began to surround myself with people who had things to lose, people who were goal-oriented and who wanted to see me win as well. I brought that same energy home with me. At first I was hard-pressed to find a decent conversation that wouldn't easily segue from thought-provoking to something that was the exact opposite.

So what I did was stay in contact with some of the guys that I'd left but had not forgotten. I eventually forged relationships with goal-driven individuals, men and women alike. Then something beautiful began to happen; my friends were being released, people that I knew had something lose and so much more to gain. We supported each other then and even to this day: my good friends Dex; Ed (Tobe); Jeremy (Diamond); Terrell (Rell); Durrell (Rell); Marvin (Nook); Theodis (J-Bone); Michael (M); Jamal ($mall$); Lamar (L); and a host of others.

I did years with these guys, and even in the midst of minor disagreements at times, the comradeship was never broken. It is so important to socialize with people who are working toward something because if ever you lose momentum, looking at them will hopefully inspire you while giving you a full head of steam. Besides, nobody wants to be left behind to deal with the looming question, What if?

Hang with Those who Hold You Accountable

While in prison I encountered a multitude of characters, some worth knowing, others worth nothing more than a greeting and well wishes. With this one particular person I met through someone else, the energy that I felt when we first met was pleasant and respectful, which prompted me to speak to him every time we passed one another after that day. The odd thing for him was that I always called him by his first name, Tarez, which is unheard of in prison for two people who are virtually strangers.

He stopped me one day and asked me, flat out, "Why you speak to me every time you see me?"

I chuckled a little and responded, "I was raised to acknowledge familiar faces, that's all."

"Oh, okay, I was just wondering," he replied cordially before he proceeded to walk away.

Those greetings led to a friendship/brotherhood that still stands to this day. Throughout our time in prison, we had countless conversations, which ran the gamut from politics to religion, from music to matrimony, from hustling in the streets to surviving and thriving in prison and thereafter. The best thing about these conversations is that Tarez didn't always agree with me whereas a lot of other people did. Even when I was saying some complete bullshit, he wasn't hearing it, there was always a *Why?* or a *What do you mean by that?* Even when I was just talking to him about doing certain things in life, he always gave me a reason to look at the totality of whatever it was so I could make a more informed choice with as little regret as possible, if any.

He beat me up in chess. I did the same to him in basketball. We walked countless times around the rec yard as he challenged my thinking, which was flawed on many days. He asked me questions and made the statements that friends should ask and make but rarely do for fear of maybe upsetting you. Tarez didn't care; he poked, prodded, questioned, and countered. Why? Because he's an individual, an independent thinker who believes that the best of two people comes out of a disagreement, not an irreconcilable one but one that causes you to think beyond your typical realm of consciousness, whether it pisses you off or not.

Tarez is a large part of the reason why I understand how important it is to have people in your life who hold you accountable for the errors in your thinking when you don't really see how deep they go. We need those people around that say, *Hey, chill the fuck out* or *Do you think that makes sense? Think about what you have to lose.*

Before you can allow someone else to hold you accountable, though, you have to put yourself in that hot seat, no matter how uncomfortable it may be. When you mess up, offer no excuses. Own the error, see how it can be fixed, and then move on and see to it that it never happens again. If you have wronged someone, and they choose to address it, but you feel justified in your actions, accept how that person feels, because in many cases the feelings are valid. Own up to your wrongdoing but never, by any means, never, make the statement, *I know I was wrong but* . . . The *but* nullifies the acknowledgment of the wrongdoing and cheapens the apology.

Accountability is 100 percent ownership and zero percent blame. We have to learn how to accept our consequences the way we accept our rewards: with the same self-respect, the same dignity, and the same open-mindedness. I have friends whom I never allow to falter on even the smallest things, such as a misspelled word in a text or being temporarily lax on accomplishing a certain thing, because I am a believer in the Butterfly Effect. We have to be ever mindful of our actions, no matter how big or small, because they can foreshadow what our future will be, believe it or not.

I had a recent conversation with a close friend about the ending of his relationship with his child's mother. We all know breakups can be difficult, but this particular situation seemed to be especially difficult for him. He expressed to me how she made him feel low, unimportant, useless, and in his words, "worthless." I explained to him that he feels all these things because he gave her permission to allow him to feel such negative things.

His response was "She changed." I asked him if she really changed, or did he ignore those negative traits that were on display toward other people while somehow thinking that he would be exempt from them in the future. I also asked if it was possible that he was so engrossed by his attraction to her that he never really took notice of who she *really* is. He told me that it was neither. I told him that it was the former but rooted in the latter.

Needless to say, he disputed what I said, in part because it is easier for us to feel wronged solely by someone else without acknowledging our part in it. I mean, LeBron James gets the two points for the spectacular dunk on those fast break alley-oop plays, but his teammate gets the assist for the sharp pass. Both are equally important, but one receives more attention. In most cases, one is deemed a highlight while both are a part of the game. So while my friend was staunch in his victim stance and newfound misogyny, I was sure to help him see his participation in overlooking signs and symbols in the beginning of their acquaintance. I'm no relationship expert, but I do know that rose-colored glasses are worn sometimes when two people meet and there's an attraction there.

He again disregarded what I said and told me that she was wrong and it is *fuck all women* from here on out. That particular perspective is simply an emotional defense mechanism, something that allows a person to cordon off their heart while pretending to be cold and indifferent. Yet all it does is reveal bitterness and mask the hurt with a thin veil that can easily be detected by someone who has been there.

I've been there. I told him that the difference between my past situation and his present one is that I was in prison. I explained to him that I experienced it in the midst of twenty-three-hour lockdown and one hour of recreation. I had nothing to distract me from my own thoughts and feelings. I paced in my cell for days; I cried for hours at a time; I couldn't focus on anything except how I felt.

I said to him that it is all relative, but I was nineteen then and he is in his forties right now. At nineteen I didn't understand the things about life that I do now, so those things were not only harder to accept but also to wrap my mind around. As we spoke he was not only combative, but he shot down all that I said. That was when I realized that when someone wants to be sad, it doesn't matter what you say, because they've convinced themselves that how they feel is how they are supposed to feel. I know better. So as I tried to hold him accountable for his actions regarding his relationship status and help him see the error in thinking, it was like trying to engage a stop sign and hoping that. It would eventually say something other than—stop.

This takes me back to self-accountability. It's the internal growth and ownership that allows us to be receptive to others' advice or corrective suggestions about our choices and ultimate behaviors. In short, people will only look in the mirror when they are ready to see their reflection; it doesn't matter how steady you hold it in front of them. But if the people around you ever enable or support the unflattering aspects of who you are, they are more than likely not your friend and don't want to see you become the best version of yourself. That same thing applies to you regarding them and your desire for their greatness.

Hang with Those Who Won't Let You Quit

Misty May and Kerri Walsh

The year was 2008, and I was on my fourth year of being in prison. One of my favorite times of the year had rolled around, the Olympic summer games. I was never a really big fan of beach volleyball until I saw Misty May and Kerri Walsh step onto the sand for the first time. There was such grit that was palpable with how they played. The take-no-prisoners, no-mercy approach they took was so profound that their opponents seemed to beat themselves before stepping on their side of the net. I watched in awe as they picked one another up mentally and at times physically when it was needed. They never let each other slack too much. In every match they had an expectation of each other's effort, which led them to a 112 match win streak going into the 2008 Summer Olympics, where they won the gold.

Watching them led me to understand how important it is to have people in your life and on your team who won't allow you to give up, Not only is it necessary to have people who won't allow you to give up, but we need to surround ourselves with people who push us to be the best version or ourselves. The impact that knowing this had on my life led me to seek out people who always pushed me to do and be better.

I want you to understand how conducive those people will be to our growth as productive individuals in life; who can not only change ourselves but our world as well. Misty May once said, "I'm stronger than I think I am. Mentally and physically." This particular statement resonated with me because no amount of mental preparation can create a sufficient amount of readiness to serve half your life in prison—or even a portion. So as I watched Misty May and Kerri Walsh topple opponent after opponent, I knocked down day after day that led to year after year and likened my daily victories on prison yards to theirs on the sand. They let nothing stop them, and I vowed to never allow anything to stop me, because I knew that I was stronger than I thought I was, mentally and physically.

Each time I wrote a song while I was in prison, numerous people would like it. For the most part, I used to call it my "heat check," the process of me seeing how hot it was. I didn't care a lot about the people who loved it already; it was the friend of mine who heard it and nonchalantly said, "It's all right," whose opinion I wanted to change. His lack of enthusiasm bothered me to no end. It was to the point that I modified some of the words to accommodate him, and I made other people who once liked it, dislike it—and he still didn't like it! He was almost the cause of me putting down my pen for good. Instead, he became the cause of me never putting it down. He asked me one day, "Are you gonna let me not liking one if your songs make you forget about me loving several other ones?"

I sat there dumbfounded as he continued, "If you can't take one undesirable opinion, then you're not ready for the life that you say you want."

I didn't care about anyone else's opinion because I respected his so much. He was absolutely right, though, and it was that statement that let me know how important the it's-all-right people are to your life. We need people who push us, but most importantly we need people who push us to push ourselves.

We Need Defeat to Feel Complete

Kevin Garnett

As I've stated numerous times regarding my story, I went to prison four times. That was four hard losses that led to me having to start anew time after time, only to lose again and again, while knowing all along in the very depths of my being that I was destined for something much greater than what was before and what seemed would be after. Something within would never allow me to completely throw in the towel, so every time I faltered or came close to where I wanted to be but still wound up not winning, for every one of my peers I watched succeed and become great, a drive was ignited in me. That newly lit drive reignited my resolve. I'm not a loser, I told myself time after time in spite of how I felt and how bleak the circumstances seemed at the moment.

The year was 2008, and I was watching the NBA finals being played by the Boston Celtics and the Los Angeles Lakers. One of my favorite players was Kobe Bryant (RIP), and I wanted him to win because they said he couldn't do it without Shaq, even though Shaq won in Miami without him in the 2005/2006 finals. On the opposing side playing for Boston was another favorite of mine, Kevin Garnett. I felt a special energetic connection with him because he was an underdog, a dark horse even, something I considered myself to be. I began watching Kevin Garnett after he was drafted by the Minnesota Timberwolves in 1995 as the youngest player ever in the NBA. I also rooted for him in 1997 as the Wolves made their first playoff appearance, only to lose in the first round by a sweep to the Houston Rockets. The following year proved just as successful with another loss in the first round, this time to Gary Payton and the Seattle Supersonics.

The 1998/1999 season had been marred by a fifty-game lockout and led to the Timberwolves having a disappointing showing, winning only twenty-five games, barely making the playoffs. They lost again in the first round, this time to the San Antonio Spurs and the likes of Tim Duncan. They were bested 3-1 in the series. Kevin Garnett never slowed in his spectacular play, but they could not seem to make it past the first round of the playoffs. The 1999/2000 season showed no difference as they lost in the first round again, this time to the Portland Trailblazers. Garnett gained a reputation for being a dominant power forward who couldn't make it out of the first round. Even in the 2000/2001 season, the Wolves boasted a 47-35 record and still lost in the first round for the second time 3-1 to the San Antonio Spurs. As disappointing as it was, Kevin knew he had to make some adjustments and get better.

In the 2001/2002 season they lost again in the first round, this time to the Dallas Mavericks. Kevin still knew that he was meant to win, so he came back stronger and better. In the 2002/2003 season they lost again, this time to the LA Lakers. In the 2003/2004 season they finally made it past the first round by beating the Denver Nuggets, but lost in the second round to the Lakers. In the 2004/2005 season they didn't make the playoffs.

Before long Kevin wanted to be traded; he'd walked that road long enough.

In the 2007/2008 season he was traded to the Boston Celtics, where he finally made it to the highly desired NBA finals. The Celtics not only played the iconic LA Lakers, they beat them in storybook fashion, which led to an incomparable post-game interview with Michele Tafoya and Kevin Garnett where he yelled the memorable phrase, "Anything is possible!"

I felt those words all the way in a tiny prison cell in Oshkosh, Wisconsin, and they guided me on the journey to writing this book.

I watched for years as Garnett never gave up, always fought, always left everything out on the floor, and still suffered loss after loss, but eventually achieved champion status via perseverance and hard work. Defeat has a way of making us better, sharper, and even more tenacious in our approach and reluctance to quit. Garnett became a champion to the world because he was already a champion within himself who refused to allow adversity to define his existence as a competitor. That's what we have to do in life: The adversity should never define us, but how we respond to it should be our way of defining ourselves.

All of Garnett's professional struggles, all the losses suffered in the first round, all the disappointment culminated in the now iconic post-championship-game interview with Michele Tafoya where he passionately yelled, "Anything is possible!" That victory, that championship, that euphoria from accomplishing his ultimate goal provided the necessary balance to every loss previously sustained. That never say die perspective, the idea of win or go home is needed. The tenacity and fight to get to that next level should be ever present in order to succeed in all that you do. Most importantly, the feeling of defeat is an integral part of our success, just as important as the victory is, because it's a frame of reference. I have relied upon that frame of reference for some time now. During all those years that I'd done, all the years I'd gone in and out of prison, I always knew that I would eventually get my life together, and like Mike Pisciotta, I would go from Prison to Prosperity. I learned that success is to manifest, not pursue. It exists within us already. We just have to believe in ourselves the way that we were taught to believe in others.

Michael Jordan lost several years in a row before winning his first ring in 1991. It took Mark Zuckerberg a full five years for Facebook to be successful after its 2004 inception. Jennifer Hudson was eliminated from American Idol in 2004 before going on to star in Dream Girls alongside Beyoncé, where she played Effie White, a role that won her an Academy Award for best supporting actress. She also won several Grammys, a Teen Choice Award, Soul Train Music Awards, and several others throughout her career.

South Africa-born Oscar Pistorius, aka "Blade Runner," had a congenital defect that led to him having both his legs amputated at eleven months old, he would later go on to become a six time gold medal winning Olympian in track and being dubbed "the fastest man with no legs." Jay-Z was turned down by every record label before he put out his debut classic, Reasonable Doubt, by himself and inked a distribution deal with Def Jam not long after its release. What followed was a string of hits, hit albums, clothes, liquor, a management company, etc. that led to him being worth a reported $1 billion at the time of this writing.

It doesn't matter how you start, it doesn't matter where you're from, or how bleak and unpromising things seem in the beginning, or if you seem to keep losing, or coming up short. You may be in prison or out of work. Here are a list of companies that were started during the Great Depression or a recession:

Proctor & Gamble
IBM
G&E
Fed Ex
Hyatt Corporation
IHOP

You may have no money; you may be homeless; without transportation; with no significant other, no close relatives, or even someone to support you in hard times.

None of it matters as long as you believe in yourself!

The number of times you lose doesn't matter because sometimes it takes setbacks to make advances. The sun matters more after the rain and the clouds are gone. That smile on your face means the most after you've experienced so many frowns. So a loss is not the opposite of a win; it's a necessary route to the appreciation of your win. Every defeat that we face, we should grow stronger and more proficient while knowing that as long as we learn from it all, we never really lose.

I learned over time to always pay attention to the positive things that truly excite the pleasure centers of your brain and spirit versus the things that drain you of your energy. For instance, in a relationship, if you find yourself in daily arguments or constant disagreements over trivial things, it may be time to walk away and try something new. If the job that you have takes more out of you than it gives to you and there's a feeling of dread before every workday, then a change of pace is needed. If the only fulfillment that you experience is monetary, do it for a time, save some money, and move on—because no salary, hourly, or overtime wage, no tenured position at a company you have no ownership in is high or prestigious enough to purchase sanity or emotional health.

I worked for a company with a relative of mine who passed away after dedicating three long years of his life to evening twelve-hour shifts, six, sometimes seven days a week. That same company donated nothing to his funeral expenses. My family buried him with no headstone and barely an identifying marker. They referred to us as "team members" at work. Every team I have been on that has lost a member lamented at some point and gave a dedication before or during the game. Not this one. In reality there should be no expectation for a job to care about you. A bit cynical, I know, but truthful nonetheless.

It is no different than going into a store to make a purchase and the customer service rep is as kind as can be until making the commission; then it's on to the next one. Employees have jobs and they do what they are paid for. May the universe forbid the employee passes away or violates company policy in a minor fashion, but if it happens, that position will be posted the next day. In the words of the nefarious, fictitious drug kingpin, Nino Brown, played by Wesley Snipes, as he talked to Scotty on the roof of a building, "It's always business, never personal."

My point is always do what brings you joy. Those things that enrich your life matter the most. Stop putting things off; ask yourself, why do tomorrow what can be done today? If you are tired of that job, then start making preparations for something different. If you're tired of being overweight, then make some changes to your diet, begin an exercise routine, and stick to it until you reach your desired weight.

If you want to be more informed, then start reading and studying as much as you want about what you want. Everything about anything has been written in a book at some time throughout history, and now there is Google. If you want to publish that book you have been talking about writing, then turn on a laptop or pick up a pen, formulate some ideas, and start writing. Understand that you have the power to change everything about who you are, the good and the bad. There's never going to be a right time to take that first step; there will always be something else going on. If you put it off now, then today will become tomorrow, tomorrow will become the next day, then next week, next month, and eventually next year. The inevitable question comes: What if? *If I had of done this* (whatever this is), *I would be somewhere else by now.* What if? a million times over. If you are anything like me, *what if* will haunt you a thousand times worse than *I tried but*

I failed. You have to prepare for the life that you say you want, harness it, and then live it! The reason? Preparing makes us ready, and doing makes us better.

Lots of people are unprepared for the life they desire so much. This is evident in many of the stories of celebrities overindulging in drug or alcohol use, spending excessively, and ultimately losing everything because many times they are not prepared for they wanted. Statistics show that the average lottery winner goes broke within the first five years of winning. Why? Unnecessary purchases and no investments, believing that the money won't run out, and realizing that money problems are the only problems that money will solve. Often we are so steeped in bills and other financial responsibilities that we think money will solve all the issues that we have. That is, until we get it and see that there are a host of other issues that being behind on rent and other bills made us blind to. Then comes the old adage, "Money can't buy happiness." It's a cliché, but it's true. The fact of the matter is, we typically think that the things we don't have will make us happy, because we know for sure that what we have already isn't doing it.

Now, don't get me wrong, money removes a huge burden if you *are* behind on bills and the kids may need food or clothing. Even if your house needs furnished, or if you need a house, the money will bring you fleeting satisfaction. If you're low on morale, morals, and principle, or if your name isn't good, it does not matter how much money you have because none of those things are for purchase, so much as they are for your purpose. The currency is always in our character and not our accounts. The pursuit of happiness is a short physical distance because happiness lies within you. But the journey to it can be a long, twisting road filled with obstacles, deception, and facades, until the mirror reflects the truth that we often don't want to face. So as you look at your current position in life, it may seem the worst to you and you may want something more, or what you consider to be better. Whatever it is that you start to do to change that position, see to it that you see it through to completion as you prepare for the life that you not only want but deserve. Understand that there is no display of courage without the sensation of fear, and you should never test waters that you are ill-equipped to swim in, but the moment that you become equipped, begin anew, and always follow through.

CHAPTER 5

LET YOUR REFLECTION CAUSE REFLECTION

In 2010 on my sixth straight year in prison, I was at a moral and mental crossroads. I was far removed from who I once was, yet I was still becoming who I am. So much of what I used to think still made sense, and so much of it made no sense at all. I was in the process of destroying and completely rebuilding my belief system. I needed a new set of morals, better principles, and a way to execute all the constructive ideas that were living in my head. I'd looked in the mirror for so many years and had difficulty accepting my predicament and the fact that I'd changed before my own eyes before I'd even realized it. It led me to understand that the very person I'd saw in the mirror caused me to reflect on and reevaluate the fact that I'd done eleven years in total and I was only twenty-eight years old. I knew something great had to be done with my life. I'd come too far and dealt with too many hardships to be content with what they call normal and the regularity of everyday life.

Always Doubt Self-Doubt

Doubt is the origin of wisdom.
—French philosopher Rene Descartes

I never wanted to be the most successful person in my group of friends. As a matter of fact, I wanted to surround myself with people who were much more successful that I am for the purpose of inspiration and motivation. So I can look at their lives in reflection of my own and say to myself, *I need to do more* or *I'm on the right track*. The funny thing is this: If ever you feel as if you're not doing enough, then you may not be doing enough, and you may want to go a little harder than what you've been going. Often we give up on things prematurely. Right at the moment when success is imminent, we become so full of doubt that we trick ourselves into quitting. Then years go by, and *what could have been* haunts us at every turn. So I'll tell you, *always doubt self-doubt!*

Our doubts are traitors, and make us lose the good we oft might win, by fearing attempt. —William Shakespeare

Receiving a twenty-five-year sentence at fifteen years old created a self-doubt within me that I never thought I would experience in life. The moment the gavel came crashing down on the sounding block filled me with so much uncertainty and uneasiness. Every possibility regarding my future was decorated with a question mark. I looked at the length of the med line in the day room; it was like a line for the new iPhone. I asked myself, Will I be one of those guys who relies heavily upon medication as a coping mechanism? How will I make it? When will I go home? At fifteen I had so many questions and even more doubts, so I just faked it and pretended as if I was okay. That façade sort of became my demeanor, my "cool pose," as Richard Majors and Janet Mancini Billson described it in their 1992 book on Black manhood in America.

A good friend of mine, Rudy Bankston, knows all too well about self-doubt and discovering that beauty within that we all have used at one time or another to combat and overcome adversity. In 1995, at eighteen years old, Rudy was charged with homicide and later sentenced to life imprisonment plus five years. He spent a number of years in Wisconsin's Supermax Correctional Institution prison in Boscobel for suspicion of a fight, before returning to the maximum-security prison in Green Bay where he had spent seven years prior to seeing Supermax. While at Boscobel, though, he'd signed up for a writer's workshop that was headed by a woman named Pat Anderson. She was a committed educator dedicated to the betterment of an interested inmates' writing skills. Over time she and Rudy developed an unlikely bond and respect for one another that led to Pat telling him in an unforeseen moment, based on his writing ability, "You do not belong in prison, Rudy."

It was an unusual statement from not only an employee of the Department of Corrections, but a white employee at that, who'd seemed to care so much. The day Rudy left Supermax, Pat appeared at his cell and told him that she would retire in a year and to "look her up."

"Okay," he responded, and he did after a year had gone by when she was no longer employed by the corrections department. They corresponded, visited, etc., and were soon plotting on his freedom together. Pat introduced him to a woman named Dr. Donna Hart-Tervalon with whom she'd shared a finalized version of Rudy's manuscript. After about a week or so, and after reading the manuscript, according to Pat, Donna's response was "There's no way I'm letting him die in prison." Shortly after that Donna began corresponding with Rudy regularly and eventually visiting as well as she and Pat dreamt of freedom right along with him.

His doubts of ever seeing the streets again began to dissipate. In 2012, Donna teamed up with Rudy's mother. They went to meet with a lawyer by the name of Robert Henak in hopes that he would agree to represent Rudy. He agreed. Robert filed the first motion to the courts in 2014, and by March 2015, two months shy of his twentieth year in prison, my friend Rudy Bankston walked away a free man after the courts commuted his life sentence to twenty-five years. Time served was the determination.

Only You Can Stop You . . . Don't Doubt It

In 1999, David Goggins was twenty-four years old, making $1,000 a month working as an exterminator and living check to check. He was also extremely overweight and out of shape at 300 pounds. His daily routine after his work shift was stopping at Steak 'n Shake to get a large milkshake. Then, according to him, he would go across the street to 7-Eleven to get a box of mini donuts, which he would "pop like Tic Tacs." After getting home he would turn on the TV and turn the volume up so high that he could hear it in the shower. That was his routine until one morning he heard an advertisement about Navy SEALS training. In his words, "Here I am listening to the TV as I'm showering, and lo and behold, this particular day, I started hearing: Navy SEALS. Toughest training. I was hearing it cut out between the water in my ears" (Goggins, 2018).

After getting out the shower, he watched the rest of the program. "I got sick of being haunted by nobody." He said he got tired of watching these shows about great people doing amazing things. "I wanted that feeling in my head that they had: of true accomplishment" (Goggins, 2018).

Having been in the Air Force from age nineteen to twenty-three, he wanted to enlist in the Navy SEALS, which required completing one of the military's most difficult training programs. The day he saw the SEALS on TV, he began calling recruiters and heard a plethora of noes until a recruiter told him to come into the office. He showed up and realized that just to apply to be a SEAL, he had to meet specific physical fitness requirements. At six-foot, one-inch, he wasn't supposed to weigh more than 191 pounds. Remember, he was 300.

That meant he had to do away with 106 pounds. Led by determination and sheer will, he went on a crazy weight-loss plan and lost the weight in less than three months. From there he had to complete SEAL training, which can be as much as thirty months long. Hell week is what they call it, the toughest mental and physical challenge, which consists of 130 hours of continuous training. David had to go through three hell weeks in one year after he suffered pneumonia and stress fractures that caused him to drop out twice. He passed on his third attempt.

As time went on he racked up accomplishment after accomplishment, going on to enter the *Guinness Book of World Records* for completing 4,030 pull-ups in seventeen hours, and becoming one of the world's top endurance athletes, having competed in more than sixty ultramarathons, triathlons, and ultratriathlons. He also wrote a best seller entitled *Can't Hurt Me: Master Your Mind and Defy the Odds.* According to him he lives as if he hasn't accomplished anything. Where doubt and low self-worth once lived, now resides an undeniably triumphant mentality that sees no obstacles or insurmountable adversity.

As I walked the prison yard for all those years and reflected on my life while analyzing other people's as well, I realized that life is similar to a good recipe. You can have all the right ingredients, but if they are not blended well, then whatever it is that you are cooking will not come out the way that it's supposed to. Everything has to be balanced. I had the information (the ingredients) at an early age, but it wasn't blended well with my actions. I always say that you can purchase cars, but you can't buy drive, and the things that we believe in we give power to. Believe in yourself and you rein in the power; disbelieve and you relinquish it.

I looked at David Goggins's life and said to myself, *How can I get that next level mentally?* He encountered and endured hell week; I found myself enduring a hellish situation, prison. Not *only* prison, but prison for nearly half my young life. At that time I was twenty-five and had served nearly a decade. I'd looked at my own accomplishments and saw nothing noteworthy . . . so I thought. What I wasn't looking at was the fact that in spite of having every imaginable reason (in my mind) to give up, something in me just wouldn't allow it to happen. So instead of *giving up*, I just kept *getting up*, every single day. I'd filled my cell with quotes, some from famous people, others I came up with myself, but all I began to live by.

The interesting thing about transformation is it happens glacially, kind of like the growth of grass. You plant the seeds, water it, and apply patience for the results. When you start working out, all you feel is soreness and pain—why? Because growth and comfort can't coexist. You feel that pain, and it makes you want to quit because we want to see results right away. *That* never happens. But since persistence is the hallmark of winners, it is a must that we stay the course so we can see those results, because as we continue to "work out," eventually they seem to just pop up. Then the real push to succeed comes out because we can see that what we are doing is beginning to pay off, so we go harder. It's similar to making two or three consecutive shots in basketball that causes the crowd to go wild. Your adrenaline begins to pump. You thrive on the success of those two shots, and it makes the next one come with ease. Even if you miss it, seeing the previous results creates a belief in the following opportunity.

We eventually learn to never confuse a single loss with a final loss. Opportunities to enhance our quality of life are all around us. We just have to take note, pay close attention, and know that as long as we walk in the direction of our goals, we *will* reach the destination sooner or later.

The Bottom Is Just a Start to the Top

Tyler Perry

The year was 2002. My cousin and I were sitting in his car in front of my aunt's, his mom's house, watching a play that I'd never seen before, *I Know I've Been Changed*. The play, for me, wasn't that good, seeing as how I'm not much of a musical lover, but I watched it anyway. I would later find out that there were many of these plays. Many of them I did like and found loads of inspiration in them. Not only were the plays fraught with great inspiration, the story of the man behind them was even more inspiring.

It wasn't until 2009 on my fifth straight year of captivity that I learned of Tyler Perry's story. I watched an episode of *The Oprah Winfrey Show* and he was the guest, I was rapt as he spoke candidly of his own molestation, homelessness, physical abuse, and the realization of the person whom he thought was his biological father was actually not. Going from such a bleak and heartbreaking existence to having an uber successful career in Hollywood with millions in the bank caused me to reevaluate and then eliminate the complaints that I made regarding my then predicament. I once heard him say, "We can do anything." Looking at him and where he came from, those four simple words were so believable that I wrote them down at the top of the notebook that I wrote my songs in. I looked within myself and felt as those words echoed throughout my being like a baritone voice in an empty auditorium.

Prison was my lowest point, homelessness was his. He worked and believed his way out of it. I vowed to do the same. And I did. Tyler Perry's life showed me that as long as you never stop believing in yourself then your circumstances will eventually change for the better. The foundation of the change of that situation is an alteration of your inner self. When you change within, the things around you will begin to take shape as well. For me Tyler Perry is the very embodiment of having courage under fire. We have to dig deeper inside ourselves when things seem the most difficult in order to come out better on the other end of the predicament. In the words of Mr. Perry, "we can do anything. As long as you look within for happiness, you will never be without it."

Sometimes the Best Option Is No Options

I'd analyzed my mental state so much over the years and studied my eyes in every mirror I looked into to try to figure out *everything* I needed to do, not just some of the things, in order to live my life as abundantly as possible postprison. I had finally moved past the stage of wanting to give up. Even though at times I would still find myself down about certain things, I would just allow that process to unfold as it was designed to do as part of the ebb and flow of life. Then I would get back to what I was supposed to be working on: me. In my mind I had one option: *win, succeed, prevail, overcome, vanquish, persevere.* For me it had become no different than if someone had tossed me into shark-infested waters and said, *Make it to shore.*

My only option was to swim because one of two things were going to happen: Either I would make it to shore, or I would be eaten alive. Whatever happened, I wouldn't sit idly while it did. I would have no options but the obvious, seeing as rule number one is self-preservation. If it's sink or swim, who would choose to sink?

Samantha Rodriguez's mother passed away from cervical cancer in 2013, when Samantha was fourteen years old, leaving her father to care for her and her five siblings. Unfortunately, three years after their mother's death, their father passed away from lymphoma, leaving the family without a primary caretaker—that is, until Samantha stepped up and assumed the role. According to her, "My reality was, I'm seventeen, but these are my siblings, and when I looked at them I knew that they were children. They're vulnerable, and they need an adult. So I became their adult" (Inside Edition, 2020). When they are at home in Orlando, Samantha is responsible for all the daily tasks, from meals and school to household work. On top of those responsibilities, she also attends college part time and works as a waitress.

Samantha's perspective is beyond positive in spite of all the obstacles she and her family have been faced with. According to her, "I get a lot of strength from my mother. I spent a lot of time with her, and I admired her so much; when we lost her I knew I wanted to be just like her in every way. That's what I wanted to do for the kids" (Inside Edition, 2020). Samantha attempts to be all she can be for her brothers and sisters. She bestows all the lessons she learned from her parents onto them. She says her parents showed her to never take anything for granted and that at the end of the day, material things don't really matter because what's given can be taken away in a heartbeat. According to her parents, she says, "The only thing that matters is love and support" (Inside Edition, 2020).

After her parents' deaths she went back to school to get her diploma in an attempt to show her siblings the importance of education. She says that she didn't know anyone who graduated high school and went to college. According to her, "When I realized that I wanted the kids to finish school and I wanted them to be successful, I was like, I need to give them that example and show them." In her words, "This is what makes me" (Inside Edition, 2020).

In Samantha's eyes there was only one option: step in to take care of her siblings as if they were her own children and rise to the occasion of the responsibility that stood before her.

Kites rise highest against the wind, not with it.
—*Winston Churchill*

Our greatest challenges in life either reveal our greatest strengths or exploit our greatest weaknesses, and at times the lack of choices creates the best opportunity for our chances at success because from the bottom we can only go up. This is the very reason why so many people who come from abject poverty wind up a success in life. In their mind life can't get any worse, so why not try?

If you can get up every day at 4 a.m. or 6 a.m. for your job to work for someone else and further their vision, then why can't you do the same for yourself? Now, of course some of us have no desire for the freedom that comes with owning our own destiny, but for those of us who do, we accept all challenges without complaint, and we understand that everybody wants to eat, but not many want to be the chef. So as Samantha Rodriguez stepped in as her siblings' caretaker, she became the chef that concocted a recipe of principles and morals for them to not only live by but for them to understand that when things seem insurmountable, that is when self-belief has to be indestructible.

As I continued my journey of betterment and self-actualization on the bumpiest road to freedom, I saw so many people fight unsuccessfully against that natural evolution that happens within us all. I realized that we lose that fight 100 percent of the time because change is inevitable. The more we attempt to cling to what was that existed within us, the more we look foolish and not fearless, and by default we reject the beauty that is in store for us. I'm sure we've all seen the guy who seems to refuse to grow up: They're mid-forties with the self-image of a twenty-five year old and the perspective of someone younger. They may know better, but their emotional immaturity won't allow them to display such a thing. This is the essence of the mental defect arrested development, which in psychology is described as being "stuck" at an emotional level of development—in short, a mental plateau.

In my experience I've seen this in numerous people in prison. In truth, I suffer from the same thing, having gone away initially at fifteen, but as they say, knowing is half the battle, and being self-aware is a necessary weapon to use in that battle. So I came to understand that growing old is mandatory but growing up can be optional unless your experiences, and the emotional trauma from said experiences, have arrested your development. Time seems to stop the day the arrest happens. As a result, from what I've seen, that trauma clarifies one's vision, causing an acute recollection of past occurrences due to facing poor choices head-on. Or the trauma of arrest completely clouds the vision, blocking recollection for the purpose of survival and self-deception, due to the lack of circumstantial acceptance, and causes an evasion of ownership and accountability.

In the latter, things are overall more difficult in life. In the former, difficulty is there, the weather is still inclement, but your sails are caught in the wind, which propels you through the turbulence onward to greatness. There's something uncanny and intimidating about the mirror—not one of those fun house mirrors that distort your image to make you laugh and feel silly, but those proverbial life mirrors that clarify who you are as a person and that have the power to make you smile and cry, all at once. The most difficult thing about those mirrors is when you are unprepared to look in them, yet they show you something about the depths of who you are that you've been ignorant to. Kind of like when you hear your voice on a recording for the first time, and it makes you say, Is that me? in unpleasant disbelief. I've looked in many of those mirrors in my life and hated it at first glance—and second glance and third, for that matter.

I wasn't ready at all to see the things about myself that others had been seeing, to see that I was really talkative, a bit of a know-it-all, an inappropriate jokester at the wrong times, somewhat of an impetuous hothead, etc. But along with all that, I am a generous person, kind, bright, driven, and purpose-filled, with many other redeeming qualities. So as I learned to be really hard on myself for all the things about me that I didn't like, I in turn learned to celebrate myself for all the things that I and other people loved as well. The road is hard a lot of times, but hard is not impossible, and even if it was, in the words of the Adidas slogan, "Impossible is nothing." Sometimes we have to throw caution to the wind and throw ourselves into the things that we deceive ourselves into thinking we are not ready for.

At times the things that we need the most in our lives we are not ready to receive. So we cling to things that we know are bad for us just to feel a sense of purpose, comfort, and wellbeing, even though subconsciously we know that growth and comfort can't coexist. Still, we fight against it without ever being in the position to be victorious regarding such a thing. Those mirrors never lie to us, even the side view mirrors on a car tell you, "Objects in mirror are closer than they appear." That object is the real you. Confucius said it best, "No matter where you go, there you are." Each time I found myself in segregation while I was in prison, it caused the very essence of reflection. It hurt on many occasions because sometimes the silence was too loud to bear and having to face my own thoughts with no distractions was a daunting task, especially when I wasn't prepared to.

Outside of physical prison, an unwillingness to face one's own thoughts is part of the reason why so many people rarely spend time alone, or they are always in relationships or under the influence of some substance. It's simply to mask or conceal some trauma or who they really are, not only from others but from themselves as well. Other people wear a conscious façade. They laugh a little harder at a subpar joke, or they "go with the flow" when deep down they want to do something else, etc. Within themselves, the façade was once conscious. But after so much practice, it becomes second nature and ultimately moves from the conscious mind to the subconscious. They no longer recognize it as being what it is—fake—because it has become real in their mind. "As a man thinketh . . . so is he" (The Holy Bible, King James Version, 1611/1987. Proverbs 23:7).

I went through the process of self-deception at one point in my life when I was running around in the street doing things that are pointless to name here, but I mistook behavior for character. I thought what I was doing was who I was. Character is described as the sum of all the qualities that make you who you are: values, morals, principles, and actions at times. Sometimes our behaviors derive from our character, but for the most part behaviors are just what we do. So because I was doing illegal things, I deceived myself into thinking that was who I was. I was wrong. Because of that thinking, my journey was much more difficult than it had to be. I have no regrets because each time I faltered I was in a position to learn from my mistakes, and by default I was in a position to teach because of them.

I learned how important it is not only to be yourself but to be true to yourself as well, and going with the flow may be the worst thing for you because that flow may be either too fast or too slow. In those quiet times in segregation, I learned that we must reflect on the past, examine the present, and create something new for ourselves for the future. Like the old adage goes, "To get something you have never had, you have to do something you have never done" (Calderón & Beltrán, 2004). If you feel you've never been happy, then do something different that will put a smile in your heart. If you've never been wealthy, make the necessary moves to make certain that your bank account reflects your happiness. If you've never been physically fit, get you a workout regimen, change your diet, and make those physical changes that you desire. If you've never traveled out of your home state, then take some time to plan a trip. If you have a habit of starting things and not seeing them through to fruition, then devote the energy to the completion of something that means something to you. If you've never had a best friend, then change your circle and begin to hang in different circles in order to meet new people you can learn from and who will enrich your life.

Your story begins at birth via biology, but it begins via chronology when you choose for it to.

Every time a correctional officer handed me a food tray through a slot while I was in segregation . . .

Every time I was unable to use a full ink pen and was given just the insert due to safety precautions . . .

Every time I was forced to shower in my cell or forced to wear the rewashed underwear of some unidentified inmate . . . or given a book off the book cart that was soiled with another inmate's dried semen, which caused the pages to stick together and prevented me from reading it . . .

Every time I was prevented from sleeping because of screams in the distance from an inmate who'd been deemed mentally unstable, segregated without the comprehension of said instability yet still penalized . . .

Every time I missed a meal; every pound I lost due to it . . .

Every picture I received that they denied me because of a peace sign that they called a gang sign due to cultural differences—and indifference along with a lack of ethic understanding or sheer racism rooted in the dislike of things that are misunderstood . . .

Every obituary I received from home . . .

I watched my oldest nephew grow from five years old to seventeen in photographs while not even knowing that my youngest nephew had been born, because of a lack of communication.

Every time my mom and stepdad came to see me, and their age was evident . . .

Every denial of parole, every time a woman whom I considered a friend walked away, every time one of my relatives deceived me into thinking they were loyal or had my best interest at heart but ultimately disappointed me, it caused the deepest reflection and helped me understand that success is the aspect of revenge that only involves you. The other individuals are simply spectators and distant commentators, who, in the fabric of your life, have simply worn out their welcome. To fully understand this is to fully understand the different levels of frequency and vibration that accompany personal growth and evolution.

Every time I experienced some unforeseen hardship or even the smallest difficulty, everything that I'd gone through seemed to come rushing back, causing me to reflect on my current circumstances. My reflections were built upon my desire for a much greater quality of life that existed beyond what the naked eye could see but not what the mind could conceive. I immersed myself in my betterment, by way of a thorough analysis of the depths of who I really was and who I was to become because of my grandiose desires of a more fulfilling life and the lack thereof of the life I had been living. I knew I not only wanted more but I deserved more, so I chose to work more until I saw the results that I wanted.

The interesting part about life in prison is, when you truly know that you are ready to be released, it seems as if that's when they rarely want to let you go. When you are truly working toward something more productive in life, that is when you are faced with the most trials, and it is when it's the most important to stay the course. It's similar to watching a runner compete in a 4x400-meter relay race and seeing exhaustion and fatigue kick in during the last leg while simultaneously seeing the beauty of determination and drive overshadow the former as they fall chest first through the finish-line ribbon to victory. That win makes pushing yourself to the limit worthwhile. The struggle to get there is the most important. Edmund Hillary and Tenzing Norgay learned much more about themselves on the side of Mount Everest than they ever did at the summit, when they became the first two to reach its peak in 1953.

Many of us start things with the most drive and enthusiasm while not realizing that what it takes to begin is vastly different than what it takes to continue.

We have to be enthusiastic about discipline, driven by perseverance and a sheer will to make the necessary sacrifices that will cause you to level up. In life we tend to look at people whom we consider successful and say to ourselves, I wanna be like that because we are only seeing the outcome. But the moment we start the journey, we realize that a lot goes into being great personally and professionally, and what we seen in that person's success that we found so attractive was preceded by a long unattractive process that discourages the average person. The road to change is the same way. Knowing what you want to have is rooted in knowing what you need to get rid of, but it begins in self-belief, which leads to self-empowerment, which ultimately leads to power. In the words of Ralph Ellison, "Power doesn't have to show off, power is confident, self-assuring, self-starting, and self-stopping, self-warming and self-justifying" (Ellison, 1952).

Ask yourself are you what you desire to be in life at this moment, and if you are not, ask yourself why. Are you living as the physical embodiment of your own compromise? If you don't like whatever answer you come up with, then change until you do. Find a path that speaks to you so loudly that you can't help but pay attention, one that keeps you awake at night for good reason and propels you throughout the day. For me that path was changing my mentality because I had been to prison four times (on pretty much the same charge or course), and I refused to make it a fifth.

Excuse Me but I Have No Excuses

Kyle Maynard

> *You complain about having no shoes*
> *until you meet a man with no feet.*

I first read this older quote in *How to Live without Fear and Worry* by K. Sri Dhammananda, and I've lived by it for some time now. Around 2012, in my eighth straight year in prison, I first read about Kyle Maynard, who was born with a condition called congenital amputation, which causes babies to be born with one or more limbs missing. In Kyle's case, he was born with all four of his limbs missing: arms missing from the elbows down, and legs missing from the knees down.

What seemed to be an insurmountable physical barrier turned out to be fuel that caused an already existing fire within him to burn brighter as he went on to make the wrestling and football teams in high school without special treatment. At the age of twenty-six, he became the first quadruple amputee to successfully climb Mount Kilimanjaro without the help of prosthetics. In 2005, he authored a book entitled *No*

Excuses that became a New York Times Best Seller. He also became a motivational speaker and an overall inspiration for anyone who took their situation for granted. I myself found a connection with his story because I'd reached the point of no longer making excuses for why I was not where I wanted to be in life. No longer did I blame other people or situations. I took total ownership and accountability for my life and the consequences that resulted from the choices I once made.

Kyle was quoted as saying, "It's not what I can do; it's what I will do." I knew that something had to change for me, so what I chose to do was make that change so that I would be in a position to not only inspire but to teach that it is not always what you know but what you apply. I eliminated all excuses and said to myself, *There is nothing that I won't do to better my life.* I knew what sacrifices needed to be made, so I made them. You have to do the same. Stop making excuses and start making moves. Nothing changes unless you do, I promise.

Kyle Maynard was born with no arms or legs, yet he managed to accomplish all that he has in his life by offering no excuses or reasons as to why something cannot be done. You were born with all your limbs, no mental defects, and no other physical restrictions, so what's your excuse? Why aren't you pursuing the things you want in life? Why are you not believing in your own innate powers? Why are you not loving yourself like you deserve to be loved? I was once told that my greatest ability is my capability, and there is nothing that I can't accomplish with a little effort, hard work, and determination. The same thing goes for you. We tend to be too focused on what can't be done than what can be. While I was in prison, I knew there were many things that I could not do because of the physical barriers, which consisted of walls and fences. So I focused on what I could do, and that was making myself better in all possible aspects. I was once my biggest obstacle, so you know what I did?

I got out of my own way and got my shit together from the inside out.

It is said that 99 percent of change is execution, 99 percent of execution is believing in yourself, and 99 percent of believing in yourself is knowing who you are and what direction you want your life to go. Sometimes listening to others about that direction and your happiness will only lead to unhappiness and disappointment. Too often we sacrifice our own happiness in an attempt to accommodate others for the purpose of perceived immediate satisfaction. Then in the long run we wind up resentful and bitter, pointing the finger at the one we attempted to please, when we are the real culprit. Strength exists in us all that unfortunately we may not discover until we face and overcome an extreme hardship. In the words of renowned American Tibetan Buddhist Pema Chodron, "Only to the extent that we expose ourselves over and over to annihilation can that which is indestructible be found in us" (1996). That strength is indestructible, and it never dies unless we allow it to.

I've witnessed many people allowing that strength to be placed on the back burner due to a lack of belief in its existence and the overwhelming pressure from hard times, which not only clouds that belief but ultimately fosters a stark disbelief. It's similar to a baby before their first step: There's so much hesitance, apprehension, fear of falling, and distrust in their ability to walk that they just stand still, mannequin-like, until someone they trust comes to pick them up. That's much like a lot of us when it comes to believing in and trusting ourselves to take that proverbial first step in life toward something great. Often we falter and never move until someone we trust comes along and "picks us up," dusts us off, and coddles us with the lie that it won't happen again. But it will happen again, and again, and more than likely again until we understand that it's the fail that helps us prevail and not the success that makes us the best.

Kyle Maynard lost his first thirty-five wrestling matches, and each time he lost, he learned something new not only about himself but about the sport and life itself. Sometimes it takes several tries for you to get to where you want to be, and giving up will only keep you where you are. What if my friend Rudy Bankston just accepted that he was going to die in prison and chose to never fight? What if Kevin Garnett had given up after that initial loss in the first round? Or if Tyler Perry chose a normal life after his first play wasn't an immediate success? We don't always make the first shot that we shoot. Even in baseball, there are three strikes, three chances to hit a home run or just get on base, and an equal amount of chances to strike out.

Life, fortunately, gives you more chances at winning, depending on the circumstances, of course; and while you may have numerous chances at winning in life, life itself is like that $25,000 half-court shot at halftime during a basketball game. You get one chance at it, so my suggestion to you is that you make it count. Focus, take your time, but don't waste it. Take it all in, relax, be appreciative, take pointers if and when needed, find comfort in your form, and *go for it!* Make or miss, just know that you did it how you saw fit. Be able to accept the results and whatever regrets, so as you make your exit you can rest easy as you reflect, knowing that there was nothing left to give because it was all poured into a belief in yourself that culminated as a perfectly imperfect shot—Life.

CHAPTER 6

GIVE WHAT YOU KNOW, AND KNOW WHAT YOU GIVE

Don't worry about the start of the race. —Usain Bolt.

When I had my probation revoked in 2004, and I was given twenty years at twenty-two years old for a crime that I'd committed when I was fifteen, all I could think about was what life would be like in 2024, with me being forty-two. Would there be flying cars like my grade school teacher told me there would be a decade before the millennium changed? Would I be so old and decrepit that I couldn't fend for myself? Would I be gray? Would I even be sane after serving twenty years? I couldn't fathom what life would be like for me after two decades in prison (as you know by now, I didn't actually serve the entire twenty). I had a hard time seeing past the end of my nose, let alone twenty years down the line. To a young man, middle age is for his parents or teachers, and according to Andy Rooney, "Death is a distant rumor to the young." I've never been good at running, no matter how good I was at track in school, so even though I had the most difficult time accepting that I had "a dub," as we called it, I never stopped facing the end of it all, and the possibilities that were ever present.

I was once told by an "old head" that prison can be one of three things, and you have the power to choose. He said it can either be a school, nursing home, or a graveyard. Admittedly, I didn't know what the hell he meant, and I halfway thought he was delusional, seeing as how he was given to long conversations with himself on any given day. To this day I still don't know how I wound up in a conversation with him, especially one where he felt the need to dispense advice. Maybe I looked green; I don't really know. It really didn't matter because he turned out to be spot on in his assessment. I watched as people aged and became incapable of caring for themselves, and I watched as some educated themselves to the point of astonishment. I even saw people who seemed to be in good health get sick and never recover. One instance, a guy I knew who was a diabetic went to segregation on a Friday, requested his medication on Saturday night, was denied because the officers believed that he was lying about needing it, and passed away Sunday morning from not having it.

A good friend of mine complained for years about having a headache. They only gave him ibuprofen, as they so often did to inmates as if it was an ultimate panacea. His headache never went away. One day he passed out on the rec yard. They rushed him to the hospital and had to perform emergency surgery on him because his headaches had been due to a cancerous brain tumor that had been growing since 2004. He fainted in 2007. The surgery was a success for the most part, and they got most of the tumor, but his motor skills on his right side were changed forever. Somebody else I knew woke up one morning with the left side of his face drooped, he had Bell's palsy, which is a sudden weakness of the muscles in one half of the face. It typically goes back to normal over time, but the sight of it is devastating for someone who was ignorant of it like I was.

I watched another guy go from a vibrant, energetic, skilled basketball player to being crippled by colon cancer, pretty much losing his ability to walk and suffering from incontinence. I'd also seen someone suffer from a six-month period of astasia from taking a flu shot (I haven't taken one since) and had to learn how to walk again. Another older guy I knew was bitten by a spider while he was asleep and developed an infection that caused a massive swelling on his eye. He was never the same again. There are so many of these stories that I could write a book on them alone.

Seeing all those things caused me to think about the three things that we worry about the most in the street: the police, other people, and getting shot. While in prison I didn't worry about getting arrested because, clearly, that was a fait accompli; I definitely didn't worry about any bullets; and I could hold my own among the people. But until seeing all these things happen and hearing all the horror stories, I had never imagined that something other than those three things could harm me. It sounds funny, but it's the truth.

I said to myself, *I have to do something*. I didn't even know what it was that I was going to do, but I knew that I didn't want to wind up in any one of the previous positions, I deceived myself into thinking that I could prevent life from happening to me, so I started working out and studying religiously. I'd read somewhere that we can't fill internal voids with external things, so I chose to adorn myself internally with things that could never be taken from me. It was then that I realized I was able to convey the most complex messages in the simplest terms with those in my circle who refused to accept the fact that the system will lock you away and throw away the key if you give them even the smallest reason. If they will allow a fifteen-year-old, to plea to a crime in court but won't allow him to purchase cigarettes or porn while incarcerated because he's a minor, then they don't give a damn about a grown man.

In my mind it became my duty to enlighten my "homeboys" because they would accept it from me. I could rap, so I was cool; I mean I was cool anyway, but that's the perspective. I was young, brash, and a little arrogant, with a heart as big as the globe. So I would learn things just to give it to them, and they didn't even realize they were learning most of the time. New words became punch lines for jokes first and eventually found their way into their vocabulary, like putting medicine in a candy wrapper. I wanted to give the intangible and irreplaceable and make intelligence cool, because as Black people we sometimes celebrate ignorance and ridicule being smart, often to simply fit in with pseudo individuals we don't really respect from the beginning.

As I attempted to bridge the gap between ignorance and sophistication among my group of friends and associates, I was still in the process of personal development as a foundation for my own evolution and for the purpose of helping others. One of the many ideas I hit upon was something I named The Four Truths of Transition, which is a four-step process of honest, reflective thoughts regarding yourself, change, correcting detrimental behaviors, and turning strengths into weaknesses.

The Four Truths of Transition

The First Truth

Ask yourself, Do I truly want to change?

This question is important because without asking and answering this, there can be no major transition due to there being no destination. It's similar to leaving home with nowhere to go and just driving around: You'll eventually run out of gas, or even worse, be fully gassed and find yourself going in circles expecting different scenery. I myself felt that I had to change because I was tired of feeling disappointed in myself and knowing that I truly deserved better than what I had been allowing in my life.

I destroyed my old belief system that had been instilled, and rebuilt my new one based on my own life experiences that led me to fully understanding the dos and dont's of certain stages in life. For instance, it is more acceptable as a teenager to be undisciplined and reckless with money while expecting someone to take care of you; I mean, after all you are still a child. That same behavior and outlook is nothing short of ridiculous as an adult with children and other responsibilities. I reflect on some of my old beliefs and principles and find myself in awe (not in a good way) at how I used to think and view the world. Life can be likened to a flight of stairs where every step is a stage that elevates you to the next until you reach the top, skipping those stairs can be dangerous and may cause you to slip and fall, although some do it with success. The younger you are, the easier it is to recover from one of those slips and falls; the older you get, the more difficult. So you have to use what you've learned on the previous steps (stages) to see to it that you take the coming ones with caution, care, and wisdom.

This is why change is good for us all, especially if the transition that you are making if toward something greater than what you are accustomed to.

"Guard your integrity as a sacred thing,
nothing is at last sacred but the integrity of your mind."
—*Ralph Waldo Emerson, "Self-Reliance"*

What Emerson said in his essay on self-reliance is rooted in the respect for your own mind, and changing from one mental state to the next for the purpose of betterment is rooted in valuing said respect; they work in conjunction. Someone I'd known for some time asked that I go out with them to a club one time after I was released from prison. I respectfully declined the invitation because I had something else to do, and if I didn't, I would have definitely gone. After I told him no, he proceeded to tell me how different I was and that I wasn't the same person from before I went away, *blah, blah, blah, blah, blah.*

His comments were meant to slight me, but I took them as a compliment because I didn't want to be seen as the person that I was before. I politely told him, "Thank you."

His expression was evident that my response was confusing: *An insult taken as a compliment? How?*

Easy, it's like calling a female dog a bitch. Simple.

I'd asked myself many times in the past if I truly wanted to change. There were a few times when the answer was no, but when it became yes, the process began immediately, and I went into overdrive with what needed to be done. So ask yourself, Do you *truly* want to change? If so, then what's stopping you? Once you figure that out, then your process can begin.

The Second Truth

Ask yourself, Why do I want to change?

I myself had one thousand reasons why. The fact was, it felt as if my life was spiraling out of control; it was just a matter of time before I entered a prison one day and never walked back out. So I knew that being there, I had to do all the things that were necessary for me to never return again, and I knew it started with me. I started over.

Sometimes we tend to believe that relocating to a new city or state is the best way to restart our life, and for some people it can be, but the reality of it is the real restart is mental. A true mind shift is the foundation to any real, substantial change in life. Everything else follows that. I mean I could be in the most glorious region of the world, but with a detrimental mindset, the same issues that I left physically will find me mentally, and all of a sudden that region will be the problem because I lack the ability to see that it is me. So I found my why, and the answer was deeper than because. I sat in my cell on many nights and allowed the walls to talk to me as disrespectfully and as truthfully as possible until it hurt. I realized that I had left a trail of poor choices that led to unwanted consequences that led to friendships being built with guys who were suffering the same consequences, and I saw that I had a stronger foundation, in terms of stability, in prison than I'd had in the free world.

Due to me going to prison at such a young age and getting caught in the cycle of recidivism, I was never able to lay a foundation in society like the average person. While my peers celebrated high school graduations in auditoriums and walked across stages, I celebrated those same graduations in mock ceremonies in prison visiting rooms. As a matter of fact, I was in segregation when my diploma was given to me underneath my cell door during mail call. I was twenty-four years old, and it was bittersweet because I had to write my mom to tell her that I finally graduated. She was ecstatic in her words when she wrote me back. Tears streamed down my face as I read the letter, sitting on the edge of the concrete slab they put a mat on and called a bed. In that moment, the predicament didn't match the feelings I experienced. I was so happy that I had made her happy that not even twenty-hour lockdown in the hole could dampen my day.

As I relished those positive feelings, it dawned on me that that is how I was supposed to feel all the time—not the anger, the frustration, the hurt, the pain, or any other negative feelings. I reverted mentally to all the necessary things that I learned from my mom and realized that the old saying, Mother knows best, has at least some validity to it. I had become something in the street that didn't come from my household. So I meshed all the new wholesome principles from my personal experiences as an adult with the wholesome ones that I was raised with. Mentally I began to rely on what was, so it could take me to what was to come.

All this became my why. The fact that people began to think that I didn't want much out of life became my why. The ones who stopped believing in me became my why. Every time I wrote someone who told me to write them but they never wrote back became my why. Every time a correctional officer spoke to me as if I was a child became my why. Every time the parole board told me no became my why. When President Obama was elected and I saw the world changing became my why. Watching my parents age as I languished in prison became my ultimate why because I wanted for them to see me be successful before their or my time expired, so I knew I had to change.

In your truths of transition what is your why? Find it, harness it, and make it as important to you as vibranium is to Black Panther.

Never be afraid to admit your mistakes, because failure only happens when you stop trying.

The Third Truth

Your weaknesses deserve more attention than your strengths.

There are certain parts of your body that are naturally stronger than others; for instance whatever your dominant hand is, you have more confidence in the usage of it and you focus less on its mobility and even the feel of it. If you work out and have a favorite exercise that you like to do (for me, that exercise is pull-ups), then you more than likely focus more on the arms, chest, and back than the weaker parts of your body, which ultimately creates an imbalance and leaves you more susceptible to injury.

Even in sports the offense is encouraged to "attack the weak side" in order to gain an advantage and ultimately win the game. So that's what you have to do to *your* weaknesses, but before you can attack them, you have to acknowledge them the way you do your strengths, with confidence and without shame, because we all have them.

For some of us a huge flaw, or weakness, is our reluctance to make the statement, *I'm wrong*. It was a major obstacle for me at one point to simply say it. I avoided it at all costs via unfounded arguments and other verbal diversion tactics because I wasn't emotionally mature enough to admit that I was fallible; even though I *knew* I was and would forever be. As I began to work through that, I started the strengthening of that weakness by making the statement, *You're right*, which by default means that I am wrong. I would purposely place myself in conversations where I would be forced to say, *You're right*. I worked at being just as confident in saying that as I was when I was right about something.

A form of mental conditioning leads to the habits that we possess, good and not so good. Fortunately, they can all be undone. Look at your habits the way you look at your muscles; when you work them out frequently, they become stronger. The first time I experimented with cigarettes when I was kid and I inhaled the smoke, I choked; the more I did it the easier it became, and before I knew it, I had a smoking habit. Luckily my willpower was much stronger than the habit I'd picked up, because while I was in prison I quit cold turkey and never looked back. I haven't smoked a cigarette since February 2009.

Why? You ask, *How?* Well, it's simple for me, to be honest. It stopped making sense to me. I asked myself, *Why would I put smoke in my lungs—for fun or habit?* I mean, after all, when people die in house fires, they rarely get burned alive. Typically they die from smoke inhalation, and I didn't want to die from smoke inhalation, house fire or not. Of course, for some people it is much more complicated than that, but that's just my take on it.

The first time I ever stole something as a kid, it was frightening and exhilarating at the same time. Just the thrill of doing something that I had no business doing caused my adrenaline to pump like never before, like free-falling several hundred feet before you decide to deploy your parachute and sail to safety, or a rollercoaster with a sudden drop that leaves that lump in your throat, or speaking with someone whom you fear and admire at the same time about a topic that's not so easy to discuss. That feeling scared me, but it also intrigued me to the point that I wanted to experience it again . . . and again, which led to a level of comfort with doing wrong that should never be attained.

Then I learned that if that level of comfort can be attained with doing wrong, it can surely be reached by doing right. So that mental conditioning can also be done by way of positivity. I had to find a way to make my adrenaline pump the way that it did when I stole something by doing something constructive. I eventually discovered it in learning to transform my weaknesses into strengths. I began only doing things that challenged me, like going an entire day without using profanity or looking someone in their eye while conversing with them, or I would only read things that led me to the dictionary several times as I was reading whatever book.

So as I learned to say that I was wrong, I also learned to say to myself, in quiet times, that I had a lot of growing to do, and order to achieve that growth I had to be truthful about my weak points. All of them.

Education is the most powerful weapon
which you can use to change the world.
—*Nelson Mandela*

To be fully educated on yourself and who you truly are as a person is one of the most special things that we can obtain. We must know ourselves better than anyone else in order to live a life as abundantly as we desire. While I was in prison I took a program called AODA (alcohol or drug addiction) which I had no business in because I didn't have a drug case, but the federal government funds those programs, so the more people that take them, the more money the department of corrections receives. That program introduced me to a concept, Johari's window (Luft & Ingham, 1955), where the illustration is an actual window with four pieces of glass representing different concepts: The first pane represents the things we know about ourselves that no one else knows; the second, the opposite of that; the third what we don't know about ourselves that other people know; the fourth being the opposite of that one. What I did was make certain that I am comprehensively aware of "me" at all times so I would no longer be a representative of number three, or four for that matter.

As time went on a lot of things that I viewed as weaknesses were simply pockets of strengths that were yet to mature. It's on us to cultivate those and make certain that they exist as they should. Similar to not being that great at a particular subject in school, the more you work at it, the better you'll become. I once thought that I hated math until I began to view it differently and realized that it is the only subject where the answers are unchanging: 4 + 4 will always equal 8, no matter who does the equation. So I looked at myself and said, *Human beings are nothing like math because we are forever changing*, but the fact that we *are* forever changing exists as an absolutism just like the answers in math equations, so philosophically, we and math have nothing in common, but the fact that we are in a constant state of evolution is just as absolute as 4 + 4 = 8.

The Fourth Truth

Let go of who you were to be become who you'll be.

Unfortunately we often hold onto things within ourselves that we know are no longer conducive to our growth, or they may have never been, but immaturity and a lack of self-awareness allowed the justification of those things to be acceptable. An example is having a disagreement with someone that you respect and staying away until you think the tension has blown over, as opposed to swallowing your pride and speaking about it like an adult because, truthfully, it's better to address than to suppress.

Robert Downey Jr

There was a time when the public believed that Robert Downey Jr's career had seen its final act. It seemed the curtain was closing on the talent that the world once enjoyed in movies like Weird Science and Chaplin, the 1992 biopic on the comedic genius Charlie Chaplin, which landed him an Academy Award nomination for Best Actor. Downey began to spiral out of control as his drug abuse and alcohol addiction began to take precedence over the quality of his work. By the time 1995 rolled around, he was reportedly smoking heroin and freebasing cocaine (the latter being what caused my parents' divorce the same year that Chaplin was released). He was arrested multiple times, leading to several stints in rehab centers, and was also sentenced to three years in prison, of which he served a year before being released. His antics continued. He wound up back in rehab, his wife left him, he was fired from the set of the Fox show Ally McBeal, wound up in debt, and was pretty much written off by Hollywood and the world at large.

That is, until 2008 rolled around, and he landed the role of billionaire superhero Tony Starks in the blockbuster film Iron Man, which put his career on the uptick and sent it into overdrive, causing the world to be seemingly oblivious to his previous drug use and foolish behavior. I watched from a cold cell in a state of inspiration and awe as Robert got his life back on track and pieced his once-fragmented career back together as if to say, I knew what I was doing all along and I never stopped believing. I myself always knew that the life I was living cycling in and out of prison was not going to last forever; it didn't matter what "they said" about me or whether or not "they" saw the beautiful things I saw for my life once that chapter was over. I believe that somewhere inside, Robert knew he would come out on the other end of his addiction and folly a better man, irrespective of it not because of it, similar to me knowing all along that I would one day put prison behind me. The thing that makes being a visionary so profound is that you are able to see things for yourself that others are incapable of seeing, which can ultimately cause them to pass judgment and write you off as another ball of wasted potential.

While not fully understanding the power of self-actualization and the belief in the application of it, a great depth of empowerment exists in letting go of the person you once were and embracing the you that is to live abundantly in the future. So whether you in the throes of an addiction the way that Robert was, or if you have been in prison for years the way I was, please know that there is nothing you are incapable of coming back from. Whenever you find yourself in the fire (struggle) never ask, Why me? The more pertinent question is Why not me? The game of life gives no exemptions for its players, and the greater the adversity, the greater the opportunity for the display of great strength. You possess the courage, so see to it that it sees you through the fire.

Michael K. Williams

Michael K. Williams is most recognized for his role as Omar Little, the gay, homicidal armed robber who robbed Baltimore drug dealers on the HBO series *The Wire*. Michael's story is one of an aspiring dancer and choreographer who was fed up with the day-to-day hustle and bustle of nine-to-five work life. He figured something had to change if he was to not only live his dream but find happiness within himself and his life choices. So in 1989, after being inspired by Janet Jackson's *Rhythm Nation 1814* video, he left Pfizer behind and followed his heart. Needless to say, he ultimately made the correct choice, even in the face of all the nay-sayers and non-believers.

As I searched Michael's story for inspiration and parallels to my own, I realized, while I languished in the bleak predicament of prison, on or about my ninth year, that what matters most is a self-belief that can't be shaken even in an earthquake of the highest magnitude. His journey says that when you are jaded by an existence that yields no sense of purpose beyond a weekly or biweekly paycheck, there has to be a change of pace for the purpose of our sanity and to be certain that our moral compass is leading us in a direction that is most conducive to our life's purpose. Mine was not at one point and time. So due to my desire for more and knowing that I deserved more than I'd been allowing myself to receive, I stepped out not only on faith but on self-belief. I decided if Michael K. Williams could walk away from his temp job and live his dream, then I can walk away from my temp position as an inmate and live as abundantly as possible without ever returning to such a dismal state of existing, while at the same time showing that no matter what the statistics and studies say, when you want more, you can have what you want if you are willing to make necessary sacrifices.

The thing that has to fully be grasped regarding Michael's story is that we all possess that thing within us that will propel us to succeed against every odd and obstacle. We just have to thoroughly search our inner being to find what we so often look for outside of ourselves. Some people may describe it as drive, ambition, uniqueness, or even a degree of giftedness. While they may not be wrong in their assessment, I simply call it the courage that carries you through the fire and leads you to an idyllic existence that can only be taken with your permission. My advice: *Never* relinquish it.

See, the you of yesterday is a foregone conclusion, and you may have already lost faith in today, but the you that tomorrow will present can be created with the keen eye of a sculpture if you would let go of what was and who you once were. Who you were got you where you are. Who you will be can help you make a phenomenal transition to an incomparable, idyllic existence that you never thought was possible when you held on to *I used to be* or *I ain't gon' never change.* Those statements are nothing but a hindrance. They only stymie and stifle growth and bring about more sadness than gladness. Do away with them now. Leave nothing up to chance and happenstance, but rest everything upon conscious effort coupled with sheer determination.

If one advances confidently in the direction of
his dreams and endeavors to live the life he has imagined,
he will meet success unexpected in common hours.
He will put some things behind, he will pass an invisible
boundary; new, universal, and more liberal laws will begin
to establish themselves around him and within him; or the
old laws be expanded, and interpreted in his favor
In a more liberal sense, and he will live with the
license of a higher order of beings.
—Henry David Thoreau

The Rules of Disengagement

Accept that You Will Outgrow Some People

The idea that I would outgrow some people was one of the most difficult things for me to accept when I was younger. I wanted all the people I cared for and loved to want as much out of life as I did. I wanted them to want to travel the world and pursue their goals, dreams, and aspirations like I planned on doing. I wanted them to want all that life had to offer, the possibilities and probabilities of self-actualized greatness, and everything in between. It turns out that most of them were content with the people that they were. I watched as many of them became their uncles, or the stepdad that their girlfriend's kids disliked who occupied the same spot on the couch every day with no desire to share the remote or be someone worthy of admiration. There was a moment in time where I believed that, because we saw how it ravaged and ruined our parents' generation, no one in my age bracket would ever fall victim to the addiction of cocaine. I was dead wrong.

I watched as my childhood friends relinquished their desire to achieve their dreams and accepted a reality that we'd once loathed and swore would never define our existence as long as there was breath in our lungs. Some of them found solace in prison, a place where they could ultimately thrive due to a lack of responsibility. They accepted that the only reason they are not successful in life is because of a physical barrier that prevents them from being more than an inmate. But deep inside they knew that the removal of that barrier would only reveal that the barrier itself was an excuse, and they had no intentions of doing what they said. It was just easier to say what they would but couldn't do.

Watching many of them struggle with drug or alcohol addiction or simply losing the desire to dream and want what so many of us once wanted as kids, before they allowed the pressures of life to weigh them down to the point of accepting mediocrity and underachievement, was hard for me to come to grips with. I learned that when you want more for someone else than they want for themselves, a burdensome undertone exists that can cause you to be distracted from your own goal for betterment.

Cutting off someone you love who is a liability is just as difficult as it is necessary. A person who was my best friend for a long period of my life wound developing an opioid addiction while I was in prison. He was one person that I really looked forward to seeing after I was released because I had waxed poetic on many incarcerated nights about how we used to "kick it" when were younger. Nostalgia drove my desire to see him even though I knew that I was no longer the person he once knew.

It was nothing like I remembered when I finally saw him. I felt something was different with him. I would soon find out that everything was because he was now a full-blown drug addict with a heavy pill habit. He had even overdosed once, leaving his three-year-old son to call 911. They came, administered naloxone (Narcan), and saved his life.

When I first saw him, I went to pick him up just so we could ride and catch up. I took him to the store so he could buy cigarettes. He came back to the car as he lit one. I told him, "You can't smoke in here."

He looked at me, baffled by what I said before he asked, "You don't smoke anymore?"

"Hell no," I responded with a slight smirk.

The funny part is, I had told him over the phone when we talked earlier that day, that I left cigarettes alone in 2009. Apparently he didn't believe me. He even offered me one after he asked if I still smoked. He stood outside of the car to finish smoking before he got in and asked me, "You really quit, huh?"

"Yup," I told him. As we rode I could tell the energy was much different than it once was. He'd called me one night at about 9 p.m. and asked if I could drop him off at work. He had to be there at 10. I had to be up for work myself at 4 a.m., so I was pushing it. But I saw that he was trying, so I got out of bed to go get him and take him to work. I got him there on time. He expressed a huge amount of gratitude, and I felt good that I was able to do something good for my friend. He completed his shift, and I called the next day to see if he needed another ride. He told me that he'd quit because he didn't want to ask anyone for a ride home.

I was pissed. I went out of my way to help him, and he dropped the ball. I called his cousin, a really good friend of mine, to tell her about it. She said, "I told you."

I hated to say it but I did. "You're right." I shook my head on the FaceTime call that we were on.

I reached to assist him on numerous other instances, but because of his addiction, they were in vain. I eventually accepted that he was no longer the person that I once knew. It hurt me dearly to know that for my own benefit, I had to disengage from him completely because he'd become more of a liability to my life than an asset.

The interesting thing about it is that he sensed that I was on a different path in life, and before I was able to completely disengage, he began to distance himself. Those who understand that you are on a new journey will eventually remove themselves from your life because the negativity in them that doesn't match your life's mission will make them feel judged and inadequate, even when they are wrong. Also, knowing that you both come from the same place and you are on a path to greatness is a constant reminder that they made poor life decisions.

Accept that Some People Will Always
Talk More Than They *Do*

Actions speak louder than words is an old adage that, for me, gained fresh legs and took on a literal meaning while I was in prison and being disappointed by the broken promises of pictures, visits, and consistent communication. I realized that lonely hearts and minds are the easiest to manipulate. I've been on both ends of the spectrum, so I know those feelings all too well, and truth be told, neither end is pleasant. I grew up in the presence of many people who always knew exactly what to say, when to say it, and how to make it sound so convincing that you would never question the validity of it—that is, until time passes, and you realize that the spoken word in many cases is more symbol than substance, similar to a political candidate who panders for votes by making promises that they know they have no intention on keeping, because winning is all that matters.

When I was a kid, one of my aunts told my mom that she didn't want her son, my cousin, to hang out with me because he was a talker and I was a doer, which ultimately meant to her that I would eventually get him in trouble. Well, I did get myself in some trouble, so maybe she was right. Still, I've always been the type who could only talk about doing something for so long before it was time to take action. Thought is action in rehearsal, and speaking about something, to me, is tantamount to rehearsing or making plans. I've always been a doer. I just did the wrong things sometimes that led to me getting in trouble. Ultimately, that characteristic led to me doing the right thing to get out of trouble, which led to me coming out on the other end of the predicament wiser and well rounded. What I did was take the same energy for mobilization that I had when I was living on the destructive side of life, and repurposed it and applied it to the constructive side. I realized the best investment we will ever make is in ourselves, and if all we ever do is talk about what needs to be done, then doing what needs to be done will take a back seat to comments and conversation.

So steer clear of the ones who want to talk you to death about what they are going to do but have no legitimate plan for how to do it, because they'll disappoint every time. And if you are the kind of person to do more talking than doing, make today your last day of having a habit of not taking action, set forth a detailed plan to change that behavior into something respectable and reliable. If I went from being a negative doer to a positive doer, then you can go from all talk to all action, and disengage from the ones who are hell bent on just saying things because they might sound good to them and they think it's what you want to hear.

The What-About-Me Syndrome

Be mindful of the individuals in your life that find it difficult to allow you to shine without inserting themselves in that radiance. For example, you are being complimented by someone for an accomplishment or something that you do rather skillfully, and that person feels the need to highlight their own accomplishments while you are receiving yours. The what-about-me aspect of that person is rooted in jealousy and maybe even envy.

That energy will drag you down faster than Warren Sapp once did quarterbacks in the NFL. The best thing to do when you detect it is to move as far as you can away from it, because it may begin as amusing, but it will eventually become a problem. On your road to personal evolution, many people, whom you least expected to possess it, will reveal the what-about-me in themselves. Also, some will attempt to pigeonhole you at a stage in life that you have moved far beyond, and when the accolades and commendations come your way, as they surely will, so will the what-about-me-ers.

Never Use Loving Someone as a reason to Accept Being Mistreated

While I was in prison I compromised my integrity a lot hoping that people I loved would stay around for as long as my heart needed them to. I spoke over the phone more timidly than usual, I was the most "understanding" even when I truly disagreed with what was being said, and I passed it off as me showing some form of appreciation for that person just being there. Even though they didn't really support me in any way, I was just happy with a phone call and the occasional letter.

Then one day something in me clicked. I'd grown tired of inconveniencing myself in an attempt at accommodating someone else, and I literally said, "Fuck this." I looked at all the pictures that I had in my room of so-called family, and I realized that I had been exaggerating the role that people played in my life. My eyes darted from picture to picture as I stood in front of the bulletin board. I spoke aloud to myself about each one, snatching them off the wall as I went: "She means nothing." "He's a liar." "She is too . . ," etc.

When I was done, all I was left with were pictures of my parents; my good friend Jamal ($mall$), whom I met there and who kept in contact with me after he was released; Malcolm X, Nelson Mandela, Assata Shakur, Angela Davis; and my grandparents. These were the people who inspired me the most at that time. Everyone else I took a Sharpie to, sent the pictures back, or just put them in the trash. I was done with the redundant deception and voluntary lies that we called "being sold dreams."

I was being as truthful with myself as I could possibly be. I didn't mean as much to those people as I had deceived myself into thinking. I had subjected myself to mistreatment based on the love that I had for them, *not* the love they had for me. Ask yourself, are you exaggerating someone's role in your life? Do you hold that person to a standard they don't live up to in reality? Our minds are so complex that we can deceive ourselves into thinking that we are loved, but the fact of the matter is we love so strongly that it just feels as if it's being reciprocated. If this is you, it's time to disengage.

As I began to feel myself evolve into the man I am today, I learned that fear limits potential. When we cling to fear, we can miss out on some of the most fulfilling aspects of life. I found myself via what I deemed the worse predicament ever, prison, but learned to pay less attention to my outer world and focus on the inner, because the outer was a direct reflection of the inner. So if I could somehow make the inner beautiful, then I was sure that the outer would follow suit.

I was right. As it stands today, I have been free for four years, six months, and one day, the longest I've gone without being an inmate since I was born until fifteen years old, when I was incarcerated and waived into the adult system. I have released a full-length music project entitled *The FacTs Of Life* under the moniker Brad FacTs, with the song "Courage Under Fire" on there, which is streaming on SoundCloud. I have released numerous music videos. I am a mentor to a bright young man I met when I was speaking at the Milwaukee Detention Center (The Juvenile Justice center), a place I had not entered since I was fifteen years old as an inmate.

I have become an author, and I am in the process of working on the follow-up to *The FacTs Of Life,* entitled *The FacTs Of Life 2: The Second Episode,* with the lead single "Feel The Fire" now streaming on Apple Music and Spotify. I am a constant ear and shoulder for the people who are going through what I've been through; my phone rings constantly due to collect calls from prison. I always said that nothing changes unless you do, and I want to represent that subculture of great men and women the right way and show that great difficulty can breed greatness if the opportunity is given. But if that opportunity is not *given,* I can assure you that it *will be taken.*

So no matter what you are facing, whatever hardship may be before you in the midst of this pandemic, whether it's joblessness or homelessness, prison or paltry pockets, it doesn't matter, because we all possess that courage that can and will bring us from under the fire.

BIBLIOGRAPHY

Alexander, M. (2010, 2012). *The New Jim Crow: Mass Incarceration in the Age of Colorblindness.* New York, NY: New Press.

Calderón, J. L., & Beltrán, R. (2004). The Phoenix has risen but has failed to thrive: Hope on the horizon for King-Drew Medical Center. *Journal of the National Medical Association, 96*(2), 160–162.

Chodron, P. (1996). *When Things Fall Apart: Heart Advice for Difficult Times.* Boulder, CO: Shambala Publications. Quoted in Maria Popova, When things fall apart: Tibetan Buddhist nun and teacher Pema Chodron on transformation through difficult times. 2017. brain pickings. https://www.brainpickings.org/2017/07/17/when-things-fall-apart-pema-chodron/

Descartes, R. (1641). Meditationes de prima philosophiae (Meditations on First Philosophy)

Douglass, F. (1881). The Color Line. *North American Review.*

Du Bois, W. E. B. (1903). Talented Tenth. In *The Negro Problem* (p. 13). New York, NY. doi:https://www.britannica.com/topic/Talented-Tenth

Emerson, R. W. (1841) Self-Reliance. 1841. Bartleby.com, Inc.

Frankl, V. (2006). *Man's Search for Meaning: An Introduction to Logotherapy*. Boston, MA: Beacon Press. (Originally published in 1946).

Goggins, D. (2018*). Can't Hurt Me: Master Your Mind and Defy the Odds*. Austin, TX: Lioncrest Publishing.

Majors, R. and Billson, J. M. (1992) *Cool Pose: The Dilemmas of Black Manhood in America*. New York, NY: Touchstone.

Marable, M., ed. (2003). Assata Shakur interview The continuity of struggle (1997), recorded in Cuba. Freedom on My Mind: The Columbia Documentary History of the African American Experience, Columbia University Press, 2003. 276.

Niagara Declaration of Principles, 1905. Yale. https://glc.yale.edu/niagaras-declaration-principles-1905

Norville, D. (2020, February). How a college student takes care of 5 younger siblings [Television series episode]. In *Inside Edition*.

Random House Webster's Dictionary, 2001.

Washington, B. T. (1895). Speech to the Atlanta Cotton States and International Exposition, Atlanta, Georgia, October 18, 1895. American RadioWorks, *Say It Plain, Say It Loud: A Century of Great African American Speeches*. http://americanradioworks.publicradio.org/features/blackspeech/btwashington.html

Wikipedia. Self-reliance, accessed 12 /11/2020. https://en.wikipedia.org/wiki/Self-Reliance

Your Courage Will Be Tested
In 1998 I was 16 years old in prison

Courage Under Fire

BRANDON JORDAN

The Exit
Leaving prison in 2016 ready to live courageously

Courage Under Fire

BRANDON JORDAN

Courage Matters
The first hug in 12 years from my mother as a free man

Courage Under Fire

BRANDON JORDAN

Use Your Courage To Encourage Others
Visiting my friend Chuck in 2019
Courage Under Fire

BRANDON JORDAN